# The History of Brazil

# From Colonization
# to Carnival

# The Land of Brazil: Geographical Wonders and Early Inhabitants

Brazil, the largest country in South America, boasts an awe-inspiring landscape and rich biodiversity. Spanning an area of approximately 8.5 million square kilometers, Brazil is home to diverse geographical features that have shaped its history and influenced the lives of its early inhabitants.

Situated in the eastern part of the continent, Brazil is bordered by the Atlantic Ocean to the east, while its vast territory extends westward, sharing borders with ten neighboring countries. This favorable position has contributed to Brazil's unique blend of cultural influences and its role as a gateway to South America.

One of the most striking geographical features of Brazil is the mighty Amazon Rainforest, which covers a significant portion of the country's territory. Often referred to as the "lungs of the world," the Amazon Rainforest is the largest tropical rainforest on Earth, home to an incredible array of plant and animal species. Its lush green canopy spreads across the Amazon Basin, nurturing countless rivers and tributaries, including the Amazon River itself, the longest river in the world by volume.

The Amazon Rainforest not only captivates with its sheer size but also contributes to Brazil's climate diversity. The country experiences a range of climates, from the humid tropical climate in the north, influenced by the Amazon Rainforest, to the semi-arid and temperate climates found in the south. These variations in climate have shaped the development of different ecosystems and supported the existence of a wide array of flora and fauna.

Long before the arrival of European explorers, Brazil was inhabited by indigenous peoples who had adapted to the diverse environments across the country. The early inhabitants of Brazil demonstrated remarkable cultural diversity, with different tribes thriving in various regions. The Tupi-Guarani, for instance, inhabited the coastal areas and played a significant role in the interactions between the indigenous populations and the Portuguese colonizers. The Kayapo, Xingu, and Yanomami were among the indigenous groups that resided in the Amazon Rainforest, embracing sustainable ways of life closely connected to the natural world.

The exploration and subsequent colonization by the Portuguese in the 16th century introduced a new chapter in Brazil's history. The Portuguese were drawn to the land by its vast resources, including valuable commodities like Brazilwood and sugarcane. The establishment of coastal settlements, such as São Vicente and Salvador, marked the early stages of Portuguese presence and set the foundation for future developments.

As the Portuguese extended their influence inland, expeditions led by explorers like Pedro Álvares Cabral and Martim Afonso de Sousa revealed the natural wonders of Brazil's interior. They encountered vast rivers, dense forests, and imposing mountain ranges, which posed challenges and opportunities for the European colonizers. The Portuguese crown divided the newly discovered territory into captaincies, granting land rights to nobles who aimed to exploit its riches and establish agricultural and mining operations.

The geographical diversity of Brazil offered both benefits and hardships. The fertile soil and favorable climate made it suitable for cultivating crops like sugarcane, which led to the establishment of large-scale plantations along the coastal regions. These plantations, worked by enslaved Africans, became the backbone of Brazil's colonial economy and played a significant role in shaping its social structure.

In the midst of these early developments, interactions between the indigenous populations and the Portuguese colonizers were complex and multifaceted. While conflicts and clashes occurred, there were also instances of cultural exchange and adaptation. The exchange of knowledge, goods, and ideas between the different groups influenced Brazil's cultural heritage, leaving lasting legacies in language, cuisine, music, and religious practices.

Brazil's geographical wonders and the presence of diverse indigenous cultures provided a foundation for the nation's history. The exploration and colonization by the Portuguese would set in motion a series of events that would shape the destiny of Brazil, making it a land of contrasts and opportunities. As we delve deeper into the history of this remarkable country, we will witness the unfolding of its captivating narrative, marked by triumphs, struggles, and an enduring spirit of resilience.

# Indigenous Cultures: Ancient Roots of Brazil

Long before the arrival of European explorers, Brazil was inhabited by indigenous peoples who had cultivated vibrant cultures and established thriving societies. These early inhabitants of Brazil had deep connections to the land, forging a profound understanding of its diverse ecosystems and living in harmony with nature.

The indigenous cultures of Brazil were incredibly diverse, with a multitude of tribes spread across the vast expanse of the country. Each tribe had its unique customs, languages, and social structures, reflecting their adaptation to the specific environments in which they resided.

In the coastal areas of Brazil, tribes such as the Tupinambá, Tupiniquim, and Guarani were prominent. These coastal tribes relied on a combination of fishing, farming, and gathering to sustain their communities. They had developed sophisticated techniques for constructing canoes and fishing nets, allowing them to navigate the rivers and oceans with ease.

Moving inland, the indigenous groups of the Amazon Rainforest were among the most diverse in the world. Tribes such as the Kayapo, Yanomami, and Xingu occupied this vast region and developed intricate systems of knowledge and survival. They possessed a deep understanding of the forest's medicinal plants, using them for healing purposes and religious ceremonies. The Amazon Rainforest provided them with sustenance, shelter, and a spiritual connection to their ancestors.

In the central plateau region of Brazil, the indigenous peoples included the Guarani, Kaingang, and Xavante, among others. These groups practiced agriculture, cultivating crops such as maize, beans, and squash. They constructed intricate systems of terraced farming and developed sustainable methods to preserve soil fertility.

The southern region of Brazil was inhabited by tribes like the Guarani, Kaingang, and Guaraní-Mbyá. These tribes had a strong agricultural focus, cultivating crops like manioc, sweet potatoes, and peanuts. They also had intricate social structures, with communal living and decision-making processes that emphasized cooperation and harmony.

The indigenous cultures of Brazil were deeply spiritual, with a strong belief in animism and the interconnectedness of all living beings. They revered nature, seeing themselves as custodians of the land rather than owners. Rituals, ceremonies, and dances played a significant role in their spiritual practices, often accompanied by mesmerizing chants and vibrant costumes.

Trade and communication networks existed among different indigenous tribes, facilitating the exchange of goods, knowledge, and cultural practices. These networks allowed for the transmission of ideas, artistic expressions, and advancements in agricultural techniques.

When the Portuguese arrived in Brazil in the 16th century, their encounter with the indigenous peoples was marked by both conflict and cultural exchange. European diseases brought by the colonizers had a devastating impact on the indigenous populations, leading to significant demographic decline. Moreover, the Portuguese sought to convert indigenous peoples to Christianity and exerted control over their lands, disrupting traditional ways of life.

Despite these challenges, many aspects of indigenous cultures have endured to the present day. The resilience of indigenous communities in Brazil is evident in their ongoing efforts to preserve their languages, traditions, and ancestral knowledge. Indigenous reserves and protected areas have been established, recognizing the importance of safeguarding their cultural heritage and the biodiversity of their ancestral lands.

Understanding the ancient roots of Brazil through the lens of its indigenous cultures allows us to appreciate the depth and complexity of its history. The indigenous peoples' connection to the land and their sustainable practices provide valuable lessons as we navigate contemporary environmental challenges. Acknowledging and honoring the contributions of indigenous cultures is essential in forging a more inclusive and sustainable future for Brazil and its diverse population.

# Portuguese Arrival: The Discovery and Early Explorations

The arrival of the Portuguese in Brazil marked a significant turning point in the country's history. Led by the ambitious spirit of exploration and the desire to expand their maritime empire, Portuguese navigators set out to discover new lands and establish trade routes to the riches of the East.

One of the most prominent figures in this era of exploration was Pedro Álvares Cabral, who is credited with the formal discovery of Brazil. In the year 1500, Cabral and his fleet, en route to India, veered off course due to navigational errors and stumbled upon the eastern shores of what is now Brazil. This encounter, initially perceived as a chance occurrence, would soon reveal the vast potential of this newly discovered land.

The Portuguese initially referred to the newly discovered land as "Ilha de Vera Cruz" (Island of the True Cross) and later as "Terra de Santa Cruz" (Land of the Holy Cross). The explorers were struck by the beauty of the coastline, the lush vegetation, and the diverse indigenous populations they encountered.

The Portuguese soon realized that this land held valuable resources, such as Brazilwood, a prized timber used for the production of dyes, and other exotic flora and fauna. The extraction and export of Brazilwood became an early focus for Portuguese economic activities in the region.

Recognizing the strategic importance of this newfound territory, the Portuguese crown dispatched subsequent expeditions to further explore and chart the coastline. Explorers like Gaspar de Lemos, Gonçalo Coelho, and Amerigo Vespucci played crucial roles in mapping the coast of Brazil and documenting their encounters with indigenous peoples.

One of the early challenges faced by the Portuguese explorers was establishing friendly relations with the indigenous populations. While interactions were not always peaceful, efforts were made to establish trade and establish alliances. Some indigenous groups, such as the Tupinambá, initially welcomed the Portuguese and engaged in trade, exchanging Brazilwood, feathers, and other local products for European goods.

As the Portuguese presence in Brazil increased, efforts were made to secure territorial control and establish permanent settlements. In 1532, Martim Afonso de Sousa, a Portuguese nobleman and explorer, founded the first Portuguese settlement in Brazil, São Vicente. This marked the beginning of a more systematic colonization effort, with the Portuguese crown dividing the newly discovered land into hereditary captaincies granted to nobles who would oversee its development.

These captaincies aimed to exploit the land's resources, promote agricultural activities, and establish economic enterprises. However, the captaincies faced numerous challenges, including conflicts with indigenous populations, inadequate resources, and limited administrative capabilities. Many of the captaincies struggled to prosper and eventually fell under the direct control of the Portuguese crown.

Despite the difficulties, the Portuguese presence in Brazil continued to expand, driven by the lure of riches, territorial ambitions, and the desire to spread Christianity. The establishment of the colony of Brazil became increasingly significant in the broader Portuguese Empire, serving as a vital link in the global trade network.

The early explorations and discoveries laid the foundation for the Portuguese colonization of Brazil. The encounter with the indigenous populations, the extraction of valuable resources, and the establishment of settlements were key factors that shaped the subsequent history of the country. The Portuguese presence would continue to evolve, with further explorations, economic ventures, and interactions with other European powers that would ultimately lead to the transformation of Brazil into a colonial power in its own right.

# The Colonial Era: From Captaincies to Portuguese Dominion

The colonial era in Brazil's history was characterized by the consolidation of Portuguese control and the establishment of a colonial system that would significantly shape the socio-political and economic landscape of the region. From the initial division of the land into captaincies to the ultimate establishment of direct Portuguese rule, this period witnessed the growth and transformation of Brazil as a Portuguese colony.

The division of Brazil into captaincies was a strategy employed by the Portuguese crown to facilitate the colonization process and encourage the exploration and development of the vast territory. The captaincies were hereditary grants of land bestowed upon Portuguese nobles and military officers, known as donatários, who were entrusted with the responsibility of promoting settlement, economic activities, and defending the territory.

However, the captaincies faced numerous challenges. The vastness of the land, the resistance of indigenous populations, and the difficulties of governance made it challenging for the donatários to effectively administer their territories. Many captaincies struggled to attract settlers and failed to achieve substantial economic growth.

In response to these challenges, the Portuguese crown began to exert greater control over Brazil, gradually centralizing power and establishing a more direct form of colonial governance. The process of consolidation began with the appointment of governors-general, who were representatives of the Portuguese crown vested with authority over multiple captaincies.

The first governor-general, Tomé de Sousa, arrived in Brazil in 1549 and established the city of Salvador as the capital of the colony. Under his administration, efforts were made to strengthen Portuguese control, promote agricultural activities, and introduce institutional structures for governance and administration.

One of the significant developments during this period was the implementation of the system of "Governorates-General." The colony was divided into several governorates, each under the jurisdiction of a governor-general. These governorates were designed to facilitate the efficient administration of the territory and enhance Portuguese control.

The colonial era in Brazil was characterized by economic exploitation, with the Portuguese crown seeking to maximize its profits from the colony. The extraction of valuable resources, such as Brazilwood, continued to be a significant economic activity, although the Portuguese authorities also encouraged the cultivation of crops like sugarcane and the establishment of plantations.

The introduction of sugarcane cultivation brought profound changes to the social and economic fabric of Brazil. Large-scale plantations, known as engenhos, emerged along the coastal regions, particularly in northeastern Brazil. These plantations relied heavily on enslaved labor, primarily drawn from Africa, to meet the growing demand for sugar production.

The institution of slavery became deeply entrenched in Brazilian society during the colonial era, shaping power dynamics, social hierarchies, and the cultural landscape. Enslaved Africans and their descendants made significant contributions to the economy, culture, and identity of Brazil, but they also endured unimaginable hardships and injustices.

Religion played a pivotal role in the colonial era, as the Portuguese sought to spread Catholicism and convert indigenous populations. Jesuit missionaries arrived in Brazil in the 16th century and established missions, known as reductions, to educate and convert indigenous peoples. The Jesuits played a significant role in shaping the early educational and religious infrastructure of Brazil.

The colonial era witnessed both conflicts and cultural exchanges between the Portuguese colonizers and the indigenous populations. Resistance to Portuguese control and the impact of colonization on indigenous societies led to conflicts and uprisings. The Guarani War (1756-1757), for example, was a notable indigenous rebellion against the encroachment of Portuguese settlers.

The process of consolidation culminated in 1750 with the signing of the Treaty of Madrid between Portugal and Spain. This treaty delineated the boundaries of their respective territories in South America, solidifying Portuguese control over Brazil and setting the stage for the future trajectory of the country.

# The Sugar Boom: Plantations and the Rise of Brazil's Economy

The sugar boom in Brazil played a pivotal role in shaping the country's economy and social structure during the colonial era. The cultivation of sugarcane and the establishment of large-scale plantations transformed Brazil into a major player in the global sugar trade, fueling economic growth and profoundly impacting various aspects of society.

The origins of sugarcane cultivation in Brazil can be traced back to the early years of Portuguese colonization. The Portuguese brought sugarcane from their Atlantic island possessions, such as Madeira and Cape Verde, and introduced it to the fertile coastal regions of Brazil. The combination of favorable climate, rich soil, and an abundance of labor, particularly through the enslavement of Africans, created ideal conditions for sugarcane production.

The cultivation of sugarcane required extensive labor and capital investment. As a result, large-scale plantations, known as engenhos, emerged along the coastal regions, particularly in the northeast of Brazil. These engenhos were highly organized agricultural enterprises that encompassed not only the cultivation of sugarcane but also the processing of the cane into sugar and the production of associated by-products such as molasses and rum.

The production process involved several stages. Fields were meticulously prepared, and sugarcane was planted in carefully arranged rows. As the cane grew, it required regular maintenance, including irrigation, weeding, and protection from pests. When the cane reached maturity, it was harvested and transported to the mill, where it was crushed to extract its juice.

The juice obtained from the crushed sugarcane was then subjected to a process of boiling and purification. The resulting concentrated liquid was transformed into crystallized sugar through a series of evaporation and crystallization steps. Skilled workers, often enslaved Africans, carried out these labor-intensive tasks, employing their expertise in the complex sugar-making techniques.

The success of the sugar industry in Brazil was closely tied to the Atlantic slave trade. The demand for labor in the sugar plantations led to a massive influx of enslaved Africans, who were forcibly brought to Brazil to work under brutal conditions. The system of slavery, deeply entrenched in Brazilian society, fueled the expansion of the sugar industry and contributed to its profitability.

The sugar boom had a profound impact on Brazil's economy. Sugar became the country's primary export commodity, generating immense wealth for the Portuguese crown and the planters who owned the engenhos. The sugar trade fostered connections with European markets, particularly Portugal, and stimulated the growth of a commercial network encompassing the Atlantic world.

The economic success of the sugar industry had far-reaching consequences. It led to the emergence of a wealthy planter elite who wielded considerable political and social influence. These planters, known as senhores de engenho, formed a powerful class that dominated the colonial society, shaping its social hierarchy and power dynamics.

The sugar boom also spurred urbanization and infrastructure development. Ports, such as Recife and Salvador, became bustling centers of trade and commerce, facilitating the export of sugar to Europe and other destinations. The need for skilled craftsmen, merchants, and professionals to support the industry led to the growth of towns and cities, creating a more complex urban landscape.

However, the sugar boom was not without its challenges. The intensive cultivation of sugarcane depleted the soil over time, necessitating the constant expansion of plantations to new areas. The reliance on enslaved labor also led to numerous uprisings and resistance from enslaved Africans, seeking to reclaim their freedom and challenge the oppressive system.

Despite these challenges, the sugar industry remained a dominant force in the Brazilian economy throughout the colonial era. It brought wealth and prosperity to some, while perpetuating immense suffering and inequality for others. The legacy of the sugar boom can still be seen in Brazil today, shaping the country's historical, economic, and social narratives.

# Dutch Occupation: The Brief Period of Dutch Rule

The Dutch occupation of parts of Brazil during the colonial era represents a significant episode in the country's history. Lasting for a relatively short period, the Dutch rule left a lasting impact on the regions they controlled and the broader colonial landscape.

The Dutch involvement in Brazil began in the early 17th century when the Dutch West India Company sought to challenge Portuguese dominance in the lucrative sugar trade. The Dutch saw an opportunity to expand their colonial empire and gain control over Brazil's valuable sugar-producing regions.

The Dutch West India Company launched military expeditions, capturing several strategic locations along the northeastern coast of Brazil. In 1630, the Dutch successfully seized control of the city of Recife, which served as a crucial hub for the sugar trade. This marked the beginning of a period of Dutch rule in northeastern Brazil that would last for approximately two decades.

Under Dutch rule, the captured territories, known as Dutch Brazil, experienced significant changes in administration, governance, and cultural influences. The Dutch introduced a more structured and organized approach to colonial administration compared to the Portuguese, implementing policies to promote economic growth and strengthen their hold on the region.

One of the notable aspects of Dutch rule in Brazil was their approach to religious tolerance. Unlike the Portuguese, who enforced Catholicism as the official religion, the Dutch allowed for greater religious freedom. This policy attracted immigrants from diverse backgrounds, including Sephardic Jews and French Calvinists, who sought refuge and economic opportunities in Dutch Brazil.

The Dutch also introduced new agricultural techniques and technologies to enhance sugar production and improve the efficiency of plantations. They implemented irrigation systems, constructed dykes, and implemented new methods of land drainage, which contributed to increased agricultural productivity in the region.

During their rule, the Dutch made efforts to strengthen their control over the captured territories and expand their influence. They established alliances with indigenous groups, seeking their support against Portuguese counterattacks. The Dutch also engaged in conflicts and skirmishes with the Portuguese forces, who were determined to regain control over their lost territories.

The Dutch occupation faced numerous challenges, both internal and external. Portuguese resistance remained fierce, and the Dutch struggled to maintain control over the vast territory they had captured. Moreover, conflicts with other European powers, including England and France, further strained the Dutch position in Brazil.

In 1654, after several years of conflict, the Dutch were ultimately expelled from Brazil. The Portuguese forces, backed by local militias and indigenous allies, managed to recapture the Dutch-held territories. The Treaty of The Hague in 1661 officially recognized Portuguese sovereignty over these territories, marking the end of the Dutch occupation.

Despite its relatively short duration, the Dutch occupation left a lasting impact on northeastern Brazil. The introduction of new agricultural techniques, the influence of diverse cultural groups, and the remnants of Dutch architecture and infrastructure are still evident in the region today.

Additionally, the Dutch occupation contributed to broader geopolitical shifts in the Atlantic world. The conflict between the Dutch and the Portuguese in Brazil was part of a larger struggle for control over colonial territories and trade routes. The Dutch presence challenged Portuguese dominance and highlighted the growing competition among European powers in the race for colonial supremacy.

The brief period of Dutch rule in Brazil represents a fascinating chapter in the country's history. While the Dutch were ultimately expelled, their occupation left indelible traces, both in the physical landscape and the collective memory of the regions they once controlled. It serves as a reminder of the complex dynamics and power struggles that characterized the colonial era in Brazil.

# Gold Rush: Minas Gerais and the Economic Transformation

The discovery of gold in the region of Minas Gerais, Brazil, in the late 17th century sparked a transformative economic boom that would have profound implications for the country. Known as the Gold Rush, this period witnessed a surge in mining activities, population growth, and the emergence of new social and economic dynamics.

The gold deposits in Minas Gerais were initially discovered by bandeirantes, explorers who ventured into the interior of Brazil in search of precious minerals and indigenous populations to enslave. These bandeirantes stumbled upon gold deposits while pursuing other objectives, setting in motion a wave of exploration and speculation.

News of the gold discovery spread rapidly, attracting fortune-seekers from various regions of Brazil and beyond. The allure of newfound wealth drew thousands of individuals to Minas Gerais, leading to a significant influx of people from diverse backgrounds, including Portuguese settlers, former slaves, indigenous peoples, and even Europeans seeking economic opportunities.

The Gold Rush brought about a rapid transformation of the region. Settlements sprang up around the goldfields, transforming Minas Gerais into a bustling frontier characterized by a frenzied search for gold. Camps and towns emerged almost overnight, and the population of the region grew exponentially.

The economic impact of the Gold Rush was immense. Gold mining became the dominant economic activity, attracting not only individual prospectors but also organized mining enterprises. These enterprises, known as mining companies, often operated with the support of financial backers and employed a significant number of laborers to extract gold from the mines.

The extraction of gold required a labor-intensive process. Initially, gold was extracted using simple techniques such as panning and manual digging. However, as mining operations became more sophisticated, the use of machinery and tools increased. Sluice boxes, cradles, and later, more advanced hydraulic systems were employed to extract gold from the mineral-rich soil.

The search for gold had profound social and demographic effects. The influx of people to the region resulted in the growth of towns and urban centers, which served as hubs for commerce, administration, and social interaction. Vila Rica, present-day Ouro Preto, emerged as the center of the gold mining region and the focal point of economic activity.

The social structure of the Gold Rush era was marked by stark inequalities. While some individuals struck it rich, accumulating vast fortunes, the majority of miners and laborers faced harsh working conditions and precarious lives. Slavery persisted during this period, with enslaved Africans and their descendants comprising a significant portion of the labor force in the mines. The wealth generated by the Gold Rush had broader implications for Brazil. The increased availability of gold led to the expansion of trade networks and the integration of Minas Gerais into the larger colonial economy. Gold was exchanged for imported goods, contributing to the growth of consumer markets and creating new opportunities for merchants and traders.

The economic prosperity of the Gold Rush era also had consequences for the colonial administration. The Portuguese crown recognized the importance of gold mining in Minas Gerais and sought to exert greater control over the region. Measures were implemented to regulate mining activities, impose taxes on gold production, and establish administrative structures to oversee the operations. As the Gold Rush progressed, the easily accessible gold deposits began to decline, leading to the exhaustion of some mines. This led miners to explore new areas and employ more advanced techniques to extract gold. The shift from alluvial mining to deeper underground mining required additional investments and expertise.

Over time, the Gold Rush gradually waned as the most easily accessible gold deposits were depleted, and the costs of extraction increased. Nevertheless, the economic impact of this transformative period in Minas Gerais left a lasting legacy. The accumulated wealth and the growth of commerce and urban centers contributed to the emergence of a local elite and the development of cultural and artistic expressions, particularly in the colonial architecture and baroque art for which the region is renowned.

The Gold Rush era represented a remarkable chapter in Brazilian history, characterized by rapid economic transformation, social dynamics, and the allure of wealth. The legacy of the Gold Rush can still be seen in the architectural treasures, cultural heritage, and the profound influence it had on shaping the socioeconomic fabric of Minas Gerais and the nation as a whole.

# The Age of Enlightenment: Intellectual and Cultural Awakening

The Age of Enlightenment, also known as the Age of Reason, was a period of intellectual and cultural awakening that profoundly influenced societies across the globe. In Brazil, this era marked a significant shift in thought and the emergence of new ideas that challenged traditional beliefs and laid the groundwork for social and political transformations.

The Enlightenment in Brazil was influenced by the broader European movement, particularly the philosophical and scientific advancements that emerged during the 17th and 18th centuries. Intellectuals, scholars, and artists began to question established authority, embrace reason and empirical observation, and advocate for the principles of liberty, equality, and progress.

One of the key figures in the Brazilian Enlightenment was José Bonifácio de Andrada e Silva, a polymath known for his contributions to various fields, including natural sciences, philosophy, and politics. Bonifácio was influenced by Enlightenment thinkers such as John Locke and Jean-Jacques Rousseau and played a significant role in promoting Enlightenment ideals in Brazil.

The spread of Enlightenment ideas in Brazil was facilitated by the establishment of institutions of higher learning and cultural societies. The Royal Academy of Sciences in Rio de Janeiro, founded in 1772, served as a center for scientific inquiry and intellectual discourse. It attracted scholars and fostered the exchange of ideas, contributing to the dissemination of Enlightenment principles.

The Enlightenment era in Brazil also saw the emergence of important literary and cultural figures who promoted intellectual and social progress. Cláudio Manuel da Costa, Tomás Antônio Gonzaga, and Basílio da Gama were among the prominent Brazilian writers known for their poetry and literary works that reflected Enlightenment ideals and themes.

Enlightenment ideas had a profound impact on various aspects of Brazilian society. They influenced discussions on political governance, social organization, and individual rights. Enlightenment thinkers advocated for representative government, the separation of powers, and the protection of individual freedoms. These ideas fueled the debates and discussions that laid the foundation for the later struggles for independence and the establishment of a new nation.

The Enlightenment era in Brazil also contributed to the questioning of traditional institutions and beliefs. The Catholic Church, which held significant power and influence, faced challenges as Enlightenment thinkers criticized religious dogma and advocated for religious tolerance. However, it is important to note that the Enlightenment did not lead to a complete rejection of religion in Brazil but rather stimulated critical thinking and the search for a more rational and inclusive understanding of spirituality.

Enlightenment ideals also had an impact on education and culture in Brazil. The promotion of reason and knowledge led to advancements in education, with an emphasis on the importance of scientific inquiry, critical thinking, and the dissemination of knowledge to the broader population. Libraries, schools, and educational societies were established, contributing to the expansion of literacy and intellectual development.

The Enlightenment era in Brazil coincided with other significant historical events, such as the American and French Revolutions. These events further fueled the spread of Enlightenment ideas and inspired discussions on political rights, social justice, and the pursuit of liberty.

While the influence of the Enlightenment was significant, its impact was not uniform throughout Brazil. The dissemination of Enlightenment ideas was largely concentrated among the intellectual and educated elites, who had access to the institutions and resources necessary to engage in these discussions. The majority of the population, particularly those in rural and marginalized communities, had limited exposure to Enlightenment thought.

The Enlightenment era in Brazil set the stage for subsequent historical developments, including the movement towards independence from Portuguese rule. The ideas of liberty, equality, and progress espoused during this period provided a framework for the debates and political movements that would shape Brazil's future.

The Age of Enlightenment in Brazil represented a period of intellectual and cultural awakening, where new ideas challenged traditional beliefs and influenced various aspects of society. Its legacy can be seen in the pursuit of knowledge, the promotion of critical thinking, and the continued pursuit of social, political, and intellectual progress in Brazil.

# In Search of Independence: Movements and Figures

The quest for independence from Portuguese rule marked a significant period in Brazil's history, characterized by the emergence of movements and figures that played instrumental roles in the country's path towards autonomy. The desire for self-determination, coupled with a growing sense of national identity, propelled Brazil towards the challenging and transformative process of seeking independence.

One of the key figures in Brazil's journey towards independence was Dom Pedro I. Born in Portugal, Dom Pedro I arrived in Brazil as the prince regent in 1808, fleeing the invasion of Napoleon's forces. Over time, he developed close ties with Brazil and its people, earning their loyalty and trust. When tensions between Brazil and Portugal escalated, Dom Pedro I took a decisive step on September 7, 1822, declaring Brazil's independence from Portugal and becoming the country's first emperor.

The events leading up to Brazil's declaration of independence were complex and multifaceted. The Napoleonic Wars and the subsequent presence of the Portuguese court in Brazil opened up new avenues for political discussions and debates about the country's future. The liberal ideas of the Enlightenment and the echoes of other independence movements around the world further fueled the desire for autonomy among Brazilians.

Brazil experienced various movements and uprisings in its search for independence. One significant event was the

"Cry of Ipiranga" in 1822, when Dom Pedro I declared independence on the banks of the Ipiranga River in São Paulo. This symbolic act galvanized support and set in motion a series of political and military actions aimed at securing Brazil's independence.

The period following the declaration of independence was marked by both internal and external challenges. Dom Pedro I faced opposition from Portuguese loyalists and faced the need to consolidate his power and establish a stable government. Additionally, regional tensions and conflicting interests complicated the process of unifying the vast territory of Brazil under a central authority.

Brazil's path to independence also involved diplomatic negotiations and international recognition. The Brazilian government, led by Dom Pedro I, actively sought recognition from other nations, aiming to establish Brazil as an independent and sovereign state. Over time, several countries, including the United States and Great Britain, recognized Brazil's independence, further solidifying its status on the world stage.

The quest for independence also involved the participation of diverse societal groups and movements. The liberal intellectuals and the military played crucial roles in advocating for and fighting for Brazil's autonomy. Figures such as Joaquim Gonçalves Ledo, José Bonifácio de Andrada e Silva, and Cipriano Barata were instrumental in shaping the political landscape and advancing the cause of independence through their writings, speeches, and organizational efforts.

The struggle for independence was not without its complexities and conflicts. Regional differences, competing political factions, and the legacy of slavery posed significant challenges. In the northeastern region, conflicts arose between supporters of independence and those who favored maintaining closer ties with Portugal. In Bahia, for instance, a bloody conflict known as the Bahian Revolution unfolded between Portuguese forces and those seeking Brazilian independence. The process of achieving independence culminated in the recognition of Brazil as an empire in 1824. A constitution was established, outlining the political structure and granting certain rights to citizens. Dom Pedro I, as the constitutional emperor, faced further challenges in governing a diverse and expansive nation, but his reign marked a crucial step in Brazil's transition towards self-governance.

The search for independence in Brazil set the stage for subsequent political developments, including the transition from a monarchy to a republic in 1889. The ideals of liberty, equality, and self-determination that underpinned the movement for independence remained essential in shaping Brazil's evolving political and social landscape.

The road to independence was a complex and multifaceted journey, involving the efforts of various figures, movements, and societal groups. While Brazil achieved formal independence in 1822, the process of building a unified nation and addressing longstanding societal issues would continue to unfold in the years and decades that followed.

The quest for independence was a pivotal moment in Brazil's history, marking a significant shift towards self-determination and nation-building. It remains a source of national pride and continues to shape Brazil's identity and aspirations as a sovereign nation.

# The Brazilian Empire: Dom Pedro I and the Birth of a Nation

The establishment of the Brazilian Empire under the reign of Dom Pedro I marked a significant period in Brazil's history, representing the birth of a nation and the consolidation of its political and social institutions. Dom Pedro I played a central role in guiding Brazil through its early years of independence, navigating the complexities of governance and shaping the foundations of the empire.

After declaring Brazil's independence from Portugal in 1822, Dom Pedro I assumed the title of Emperor of Brazil. As the country's first emperor, he faced the immense task of uniting a vast territory and establishing a stable government. Dom Pedro I sought to consolidate his power and create a sense of national identity among the diverse population of Brazil.

One of the key challenges for Dom Pedro I was to establish a constitution that would govern the newly independent Brazil. The Constitution of 1824 was adopted, outlining the political structure of the empire and defining the rights and obligations of citizens. This constitution established a constitutional monarchy, granting certain powers to the emperor while also providing for representative institutions such as the General Assembly and the Senate.

Dom Pedro I's reign was marked by efforts to modernize and develop Brazil's infrastructure and institutions. He promoted economic growth, encouraging industrialization, expanding trade, and fostering foreign investments. Public works projects, such as the construction of roads, bridges, and ports, aimed to improve transportation and facilitate commerce. Dom Pedro I also invested in education and cultural development, recognizing the importance of knowledge and intellectual advancement for the progress of the nation.

However, the reign of Dom Pedro I was not without challenges and controversies. Internal conflicts and political tensions, exacerbated by regional differences and personal ambitions, posed significant obstacles to the stability of the empire. Opposition movements, such as the Confederation of the Equator in the Northeast and the Republican Movement in the South, emerged, challenging the authority of the emperor and advocating for alternative forms of government.

One of the notable crises during Dom Pedro I's reign was the conflict with Portugal over the recognition of Brazil's independence. Relations between Brazil and Portugal remained strained, and tensions escalated in 1825 when Portugal attempted to reclaim control over Brazil. The ensuing conflict, known as the Cisplatine War, resulted in Brazil retaining control over the Banda Oriental, present-day Uruguay, and further solidified Brazil's position as an independent nation.

The reign of Dom Pedro I came to an end in 1831 when he abdicated the throne in favor of his young son, Dom Pedro II. His decision was influenced by various factors, including growing opposition, political instability, and personal motivations. Dom Pedro I's abdication marked a crucial transition in Brazil's monarchy and set the stage for the subsequent rule of Dom Pedro II, who would become one of Brazil's longest-serving and influential monarchs.

The Brazilian Empire under Dom Pedro I laid the groundwork for the nation's political and institutional development. Despite the challenges faced during his reign, his efforts to consolidate power, promote economic growth, and establish a constitutional framework were crucial in shaping the early years of Brazilian independence. Dom Pedro I's legacy as the first emperor of Brazil remains an important chapter in the country's history, representing a period of nation-building and the establishment of fundamental institutions.

The Brazilian Empire under Dom Pedro I provided a platform for Brazil to assert itself as a sovereign nation and navigate the complexities of governance. The developments and policies initiated during his reign set the stage for Brazil's continued evolution as a nation and the subsequent transition to a republican form of government in 1889.

The legacy of Dom Pedro I and the Brazilian Empire encompasses both achievements and challenges, illustrating the complexities of nation-building and the journey towards a stable and cohesive society. His reign as the first emperor of Brazil stands as a testament to the efforts to forge a national identity and establish the foundations of a newly independent nation.

# Coffee and Rubber: Economic Booms and Transformation

The cultivation of coffee and rubber in Brazil during the late 19th and early 20th centuries brought about significant economic booms and transformative changes in the country. These commodities, fueled by growing global demand, played instrumental roles in shaping Brazil's economy, society, and territorial expansion.

The coffee industry emerged as a dominant force in Brazil's economy during the 19th century. Coffee cultivation initially gained prominence in the regions of Rio de Janeiro and São Paulo, where favorable climatic conditions and fertile soil provided ideal conditions for its growth. The demand for coffee in Europe and North America skyrocketed, fueling the expansion of coffee plantations and propelling Brazil to become the world's largest producer.

The cultivation of coffee required extensive labor and capital investment. Large-scale plantations, known as fazendas, were established, covering vast stretches of land and employing a substantial workforce. Immigrants from various parts of the world, including Europe and Asia, were brought to Brazil to work on the coffee plantations, contributing to the cultural diversity and demographic shifts in the country.

The success of the coffee industry had profound effects on Brazil's economy. It became a major export commodity, generating substantial wealth and contributing to the country's economic growth. Coffee revenues fueled investments in infrastructure development, such as the construction of railways and the modernization of ports, which facilitated the transportation and export of coffee to international markets.

The economic prosperity generated by the coffee industry also led to significant social transformations. The expansion of coffee plantations created a new class of wealthy landowners and entrepreneurs who wielded considerable economic and political influence. This emergent elite, often referred to as the coffee barons, shaped the social fabric of Brazil, influencing politics, cultural life, and urban development.

The coffee boom had implications for territorial expansion as well. The expanding coffee plantations pushed the agricultural frontier into previously unsettled regions, particularly in the states of Paraná, Minas Gerais, and Espírito Santo. This expansion led to the clearing of land for coffee cultivation and the establishment of new settlements, further contributing to Brazil's territorial growth.

While the coffee industry brought wealth and prosperity to some, it also perpetuated significant social inequalities. The reliance on cheap labor, including the extensive use of enslaved individuals and later, impoverished workers, created exploitative working conditions and entrenched social hierarchies. The concentration of land ownership and economic power in the hands of a few exacerbated existing inequalities, leaving many Brazilians marginalized and economically disadvantaged.

In addition to coffee, rubber emerged as another significant economic driver in Brazil during the late 19th and early

20th centuries. The Amazon region, particularly the states of Amazonas and Pará, became centers of rubber production. The demand for rubber, driven by the rapid industrialization in Europe and North America, fueled the expansion of rubber plantations and the exploitation of the Amazon's vast rubber tree forests.

Rubber extraction required skilled laborers to tap rubber trees and collect latex, which was then processed into rubber. Indigenous communities and migrants from various parts of Brazil, as well as from other countries such as Portugal and Italy, were drawn to the rubber-rich regions, contributing to the cultural diversity and the formation of rubber-based economies.

The rubber boom led to the rapid growth of cities such as Manaus and Belém, which served as major rubber trading centers. The wealth generated from rubber production transformed these cities into bustling urban hubs, characterized by opulent architecture, cultural vibrancy, and the influx of foreign goods and influences.

However, the rubber industry's boom was short-lived. The discovery of rubber tree plantations in other parts of the world, particularly in Southeast Asia, led to a decline in rubber prices, making Brazilian rubber less competitive in the global market. The collapse of the rubber industry in Brazil brought economic hardships and social disruptions to the regions dependent on rubber production.

The coffee and rubber booms profoundly shaped Brazil's economic, social, and territorial landscape during the late 19th and early 20th centuries. The wealth generated by these industries contributed to the modernization of Brazil, stimulating urban development, infrastructure projects, and cultural advancements. However, the legacies of these booms are also intertwined with the perpetuation of social inequalities, exploitative labor practices, and the vulnerability of mono-export economies.

The coffee and rubber industries represented pivotal chapters in Brazil's economic history, illustrating the dynamics of global market forces, the interplay between agricultural production and territorial expansion, and the complex social and economic consequences of these economic booms.

# Abolitionism and the End of Slavery: Social Struggles and Achievements

The movement to abolish slavery in Brazil represented a significant chapter in the nation's history, marked by social struggles, shifting attitudes, and the ultimate achievement of emancipation. The abolitionist movement emerged as a response to the deep-seated inequalities and human rights violations perpetuated by the institution of slavery.

Slavery was deeply entrenched in Brazil, with the country being the largest importer of enslaved Africans during the transatlantic slave trade. The enslaved population formed an integral part of Brazil's labor force, working primarily in agriculture, mining, and domestic service. Slavery played a central role in the country's economic development, but it also resulted in the dehumanization, exploitation, and suffering of millions of individuals.

The early voices advocating for the abolition of slavery in Brazil emerged during the late 18th century, influenced by the ideals of the Enlightenment and the growing international sentiment against the institution of slavery. These early abolitionists, such as José Bonifácio de Andrada e Silva, highlighted the moral and ethical concerns surrounding slavery and called for its gradual abolition.

However, it was not until the 19th century that the abolitionist movement gained momentum and began to challenge the status quo more forcefully. Influenced by the wider abolitionist movements around the world, Brazilian abolitionists organized societies, published newspapers and pamphlets, and engaged in public debates to raise awareness about the injustices of slavery.

The abolitionist movement in Brazil gained traction as the 19th century progressed, buoyed by a combination of factors. The increasing influence of liberal and humanitarian ideas, the growth of urban centers, and the changing economic landscape all contributed to the growing opposition to slavery. The movement attracted support from diverse segments of society, including intellectuals, religious leaders, and former slaves themselves.

The struggle for abolition was not without obstacles and resistance. Slaveholders and proponents of slavery defended their interests and perpetuated the myth of racial superiority to justify the institution. They argued that the economy would collapse without the labor provided by enslaved individuals and sought to maintain their power and economic advantage.

Despite these challenges, the abolitionist movement in Brazil achieved significant milestones. The Lei Eusébio de Queirós, passed in 1850, banned the transatlantic slave trade, cutting off the supply of newly enslaved Africans. This marked a crucial step towards the eventual eradication of slavery in Brazil.

Another milestone came with the passage of the Lei Áurea, or the Golden Law, in 1888. This law, signed by Princess Isabel, officially abolished slavery in Brazil. It represented a historic moment of triumph for the abolitionist movement and the result of years of struggle and advocacy. Brazil became the last country in the Americas to abolish slavery, freeing approximately four million enslaved individuals.

The end of slavery in Brazil had far-reaching consequences. It brought about significant changes in the social fabric of the country, challenging the deeply ingrained racial hierarchy and paving the way for new possibilities for formerly enslaved individuals. The legacy of slavery, however, continued to shape Brazilian society, as racial inequalities and discrimination persisted.

The abolitionist movement and the ultimate achievement of emancipation in Brazil represented a transformative period in the nation's history. It symbolized a collective effort to rectify the injustices of the past and to recognize the inherent dignity and rights of all individuals, regardless of their race or background.

The struggle for abolition serves as a reminder of the power of social movements, advocacy, and collective action in effecting positive change. The achievements of the abolitionist movement in Brazil stand as a testament to the resilience, determination, and courage of those who fought against the oppressive institution of slavery, contributing to the ongoing quest for equality and social justice in the country.

# The Republic Era: Political Instability and Modernization

The establishment of the Republic in Brazil marked a significant period in the nation's history, characterized by political instability, societal changes, and attempts at modernization. The transition from a monarchy to a republic brought about profound transformations in Brazil's political landscape, as well as efforts to adapt to the challenges and opportunities of the modern era.

The Republic was officially proclaimed in Brazil on November 15, 1889, following the abdication of Dom Pedro II. The republican movement gained momentum as discontent grew with the monarchy's perceived failures and an increasing desire for political and social change. The establishment of the Republic represented an attempt to break away from the monarchical past and establish a more democratic and progressive system of governance.

However, the early years of the Republic were marked by political instability and frequent changes in leadership. The country experienced a series of political upheavals, including a succession of provisional governments and military interventions. Different factions and regional interests vied for power, leading to a lack of political stability and prolonged periods of uncertainty.

The instability of the Republic era was further compounded by social and economic challenges. Brazil faced significant socioeconomic disparities, with deep inequalities and widespread poverty. Attempts were made to address these issues through social reforms and modernization efforts, but progress was often hindered by political instability and vested interests.

During this era, Brazil underwent a process of modernization, particularly in urban areas. The growth of cities, such as Rio de Janeiro and São Paulo, accelerated, fueled by industrialization and rural-to-urban migration. Infrastructure projects, including the construction of railways, paved roads, and public utilities, aimed to improve transportation and provide basic services to urban residents.

Modernization efforts also extended to education and cultural development. The establishment of public schools and universities sought to expand access to education and promote intellectual advancement. The arts, literature, and scientific research flourished, reflecting the intellectual vibrancy of the era and the emergence of new ideas and expressions.

The Republic era witnessed attempts to implement social and labor reforms. Efforts were made to improve working conditions, regulate labor relations, and address social inequality. However, progress in these areas was often slow and uneven, as political divisions and competing interests hindered the implementation of comprehensive reforms.

Political factions, such as the positivists and the military, played influential roles during the Republic era. The positivists advocated for a technocratic government guided by scientific principles, while the military exerted significant influence through their involvement in political affairs and periodic interventions. These factions shaped the political discourse and policies of the era, but their influence also contributed to political polarization and further instability.

The Republic era in Brazil was also marked by the consolidation of democratic institutions. The Constitution of 1891 established the framework for the new republic, outlining the separation of powers, individual rights, and the formation of representative bodies. However, the democratic system faced numerous challenges, including limitations on suffrage, political corruption, and the exclusion of certain social groups from participating fully in the political process.

Despite the political and social challenges, the Republic era laid the groundwork for Brazil's future development. The efforts towards modernization, industrialization, and the expansion of educational opportunities provided a foundation for the country's socioeconomic progress in the decades to come.

The Republic era represents a complex period in Brazil's history, marked by both achievements and challenges. It reflects the aspirations for democratic governance, social progress, and modernization, as well as the struggles inherent in transitioning from a monarchical system to a republic. The legacy of the Republic era continues to shape Brazil's political landscape and serves as a reminder of the ongoing quest for stability, inclusivity, and effective governance.

# The First World War and Brazil's Role: Participation and Impact

The First World War, which raged from 1914 to 1918, had far-reaching consequences around the globe. While Brazil was geographically distant from the epicenter of the conflict, the war had a notable impact on the country and its involvement played a significant role in shaping Brazil's role on the international stage.

At the outbreak of the war, Brazil initially adopted a neutral position. The government under President Venceslau Brás sought to maintain a policy of non-intervention, prioritizing the country's economic interests and avoiding direct involvement in the conflict. However, Brazil's stance shifted as the war progressed, influenced by a combination of factors.

One of the key factors that influenced Brazil's entry into the war was the German policy of unrestricted submarine warfare. German U-boats targeted and sank Brazilian merchant ships, leading to the loss of Brazilian lives and the destruction of valuable cargo. These incidents provoked public outrage and pushed Brazil closer to the side of the Allied Powers.

In October 1917, Brazil officially declared war on Germany and its allies, joining the side of the Allies. The decision to enter the war was also motivated by diplomatic considerations, as Brazil sought to strengthen its ties with the United States and other Allied nations, hoping to enhance its position and influence in the post-war world.

Brazil's participation in the war was primarily naval in nature. The Brazilian Navy played a crucial role in patrolling and protecting shipping routes in the Atlantic Ocean. Brazilian warships were deployed to escort convoys, safeguard merchant vessels, and deter German submarine attacks. The participation of the Brazilian Navy in these operations helped ensure the safe passage of vital supplies and resources to the Allied forces.

Brazil also made efforts to contribute to the war on land. The Brazilian Expeditionary Force (BEF) was created in 1943 and consisted of an infantry division, an aviation group, and a medical unit. The BEF was deployed to the Italian front in 1944, joining Allied forces in their campaign against Axis powers. The Brazilian soldiers fought alongside American, British, and other Allied troops, making significant contributions to the war effort.

Brazil's participation in the war had several impacts, both domestically and internationally. It fostered a sense of national unity and patriotism among Brazilians, as the country rallied behind the cause of the Allies. The war also brought about technological advancements and military modernization in Brazil, as the armed forces sought to adapt to the demands of modern warfare.

Internationally, Brazil's involvement in the war elevated its status and increased its visibility on the world stage. The country's contribution to the Allied cause was recognized and appreciated by other nations, enhancing Brazil's reputation as a responsible global actor. This newfound recognition had implications for Brazil's future diplomatic and trade relations, as it sought to expand its international influence in the post-war era.

The end of the war brought about changes and challenges for Brazil. The post-war period witnessed a decline in international demand for Brazilian commodities, such as coffee and rubber, leading to economic difficulties. The return of Brazilian soldiers from the frontlines also posed social and economic challenges, as the country faced the task of reintegrating these veterans into civilian life.

Overall, Brazil's participation in the First World War represented a significant moment in the country's history. It demonstrated Brazil's willingness to contribute to international peace and security and marked an important step in Brazil's emergence as a regional and global player. The impacts of the war, both in terms of domestic changes and international recognition, would continue to shape Brazil's trajectory in the years that followed.

# Vargas Era: Getúlio Vargas and the Estado Novo

The Vargas Era, named after its central figure Getúlio Vargas, represents a significant period in Brazilian history characterized by political transformations, social reforms, and an authoritarian regime known as the Estado Novo. Getúlio Vargas's political career spanned multiple decades, leaving a lasting impact on Brazil's political and social landscape.

Getúlio Vargas first came to power in 1930 through a military coup, overthrowing the ruling oligarchy and ending the dominance of the traditional political elite. Initially, he assumed the role of provisional president, but his strong political support and populist appeal allowed him to consolidate power and implement sweeping changes.

One of the key aspects of the Vargas Era was the implementation of social and labor reforms. Vargas sought to address social inequalities and improve the living conditions of the working class. Labor legislation was enacted, providing workers with benefits such as the establishment of an eight-hour workday, paid vacation, and maternity leave. These reforms marked a significant departure from the previous laissez-faire approach to labor relations.

The Vargas Era also witnessed the emergence of a strong state apparatus. Vargas believed in an active and interventionist government, aiming to strengthen the role of the state in the economy and society. State-owned companies were established in key sectors such as energy, transportation, and telecommunications, reflecting Vargas's vision of a strong state-led development.

In 1937, Vargas implemented the Estado Novo, an authoritarian regime characterized by the centralization of power and restrictions on political freedoms. The Estado Novo dissolved the existing legislative bodies and concentrated power in the hands of the executive branch. Vargas justified this authoritarian turn by citing the need for stability and order in a time of national crisis.

During the Estado Novo, Vargas maintained control through a mix of populist policies, propaganda, and repression. He sought to build a cult of personality, portraying himself as the father of the nation and a champion of the working class. The regime employed nationalist rhetoric, emphasizing the idea of a unified Brazil and promoting a sense of national identity.

Vargas's regime also pursued economic and industrial development. His government implemented policies aimed at diversifying the economy, promoting industrialization, and fostering economic self-sufficiency. The National Industrialization Plan (Plano de Metas) sought to stimulate domestic industries and reduce dependency on foreign imports.

The Vargas Era was not without controversy and opposition. Political dissent was suppressed, and opposition leaders were persecuted or silenced. Vargas's regime faced challenges from various groups, including leftist movements, military factions, and conservative forces. Despite these challenges, Vargas managed to maintain his grip on power, partly due to his ability to navigate between different political forces.

The Vargas Era came to an end in 1945 with Vargas's resignation following increased pressure from the military and civilian opposition. However, Vargas returned to power through democratic means in 1951, serving as president until 1954 when he took his own life in a moment of personal and political crisis.

The legacy of the Vargas Era remains complex and subject to interpretation. Some view Vargas as a transformative leader who modernized Brazil, implemented progressive social reforms, and championed national development. Others criticize his authoritarian methods and his suppression of democratic institutions and political freedoms.

The Vargas Era represents a period of political and social change in Brazil's history. It highlights the tensions between democratic aspirations and authoritarian tendencies, the struggle for social justice, and the challenges of nation-building. The impact of Vargas's policies and the Estado Novo continues to shape Brazil's political discourse and the ongoing debate about the role of the state, social reforms, and the balance between individual freedoms and the collective good.

# World War II and Brazil's Contribution: The Battle of the Atlantic

World War II, a global conflict that lasted from 1939 to 1945, had a significant impact on Brazil and its role in the international arena. Although geographically distant from the main theaters of war, Brazil played a crucial role in the Battle of the Atlantic, making substantial contributions to the Allied effort in the fight against German U-boats and ensuring the safety of vital shipping routes.

At the outbreak of World War II, Brazil declared its neutrality, aiming to safeguard its territorial integrity and economic interests. However, as the conflict intensified and the importance of the Atlantic shipping routes became evident, Brazil's involvement in the Battle of the Atlantic became inevitable.

The Battle of the Atlantic was a protracted naval campaign fought primarily in the Atlantic Ocean, focusing on the control of shipping lanes and the protection of convoys from German U-boat attacks. Brazil, as a country with an extensive coastline and a strategic position in the South Atlantic, became a key player in this battle.

Brazil's contribution to the Battle of the Atlantic came in the form of its navy, the Brazilian Navy (Marinha do Brasil). The Brazilian Navy deployed warships and naval aircraft to escort convoys, patrol shipping routes, and provide protection against German submarines. The presence of Brazilian warships not only deterred U-boat attacks but also helped safeguard the transportation of vital supplies and resources to the Allied forces.

One of the most notable episodes involving Brazil's participation in the Battle of the Atlantic was the sinking of German U-boat U-199 by the Brazilian Navy's cruiser Bahia on July 31, 1943. This marked the only confirmed sinking of a German U-boat by a South American country during World War II.

Brazil's involvement in the Battle of the Atlantic extended beyond naval operations. The country also played a significant role in providing logistical support to the Allied forces. Brazilian ports, such as Rio de Janeiro, Recife, and Salvador, became important hubs for the assembly, maintenance, and resupply of Allied naval vessels.

Furthermore, Brazil's industrial capacity was mobilized to support the war effort. The country produced and supplied essential goods and materials to the Allies, including rubber, coffee, minerals, and other strategic resources. Brazil's contribution in this regard helped alleviate shortages and bolstered the Allied war effort.

Brazil's participation in the Battle of the Atlantic was not without risks and sacrifices. The country faced German submarine attacks along its coastline, leading to the loss of Brazilian lives and the destruction of merchant ships. These incidents heightened the determination of Brazil to contribute to the Allied cause and reinforced the need for a robust naval defense.

The Battle of the Atlantic had a profound impact on Brazil's national consciousness and its perception of its role in the international community. The conflict demonstrated

Brazil's capacity to defend its maritime interests and participate actively in global affairs. It also solidified Brazil's commitment to upholding international maritime law and the principles of freedom of navigation.

Moreover, Brazil's involvement in the Battle of the Atlantic helped shape its post-war trajectory. It positioned the country as an important regional power and paved the way for increased cooperation with the United States and other Allied nations. Brazil's contributions during the war fostered closer diplomatic and military ties, influencing its subsequent foreign policy and regional leadership in South America.

The Battle of the Atlantic was a challenging and complex campaign, with far-reaching implications for Brazil and the Allied forces. Brazil's commitment to securing vital shipping routes and its contributions to the Allied war effort played a significant role in ensuring the success of the overall campaign.

The contributions made by Brazil during World War II, particularly in the Battle of the Atlantic, continue to be acknowledged and recognized. The courage and determination displayed by Brazilian naval forces and the sacrifices made by the Brazilian people contribute to the broader narrative of international cooperation and the collective efforts to secure victory in World War II.

# The Birth of Brasília: Modernism and Architectural Marvels

The birth of Brasília, the capital city of Brazil, stands as a testament to the vision of modernism and the pursuit of architectural innovation. This planned city, located in the heart of the country, was designed to embody the ideals of progress, efficiency, and social harmony.

The idea of constructing a new capital for Brazil emerged as early as the late 19th century, but it was not until the mid-20th century that concrete plans for Brasília began to take shape. The visionary behind this ambitious project was President Juscelino Kubitschek, who sought to create a modern, purpose-built capital that would symbolize Brazil's aspirations for the future.

To bring this vision to life, Kubitschek enlisted the renowned Brazilian architect Oscar Niemeyer and urban planner Lúcio Costa. Niemeyer's distinctive modernist style, characterized by sweeping curves and bold, asymmetrical forms, became a defining feature of Brasília's architecture.

Construction of Brasília began in 1956, and the city was inaugurated as Brazil's new capital on April 21, 1960. The entire process of planning and building Brasília was an extraordinary feat of engineering and urban design. Vast stretches of undeveloped land were transformed into a meticulously planned city, carefully organized into functional sectors and interconnected by wide, expansive avenues.

The layout of Brasília follows a unique design known as the "plano piloto," or pilot plan, conceived by Lúcio Costa. The plan resembles an airplane or a bird in flight when viewed from above, with two main axes intersecting at the city's central square, the Praça dos Três Poderes. This symbolic layout reflects the harmonious integration of the city's political, administrative, and social functions.

At the heart of Brasília's architecture is the impressive ensemble of buildings designed by Oscar Niemeyer. The most iconic structure is the Metropolitan Cathedral of Brasília, a hyperboloid-shaped concrete edifice that rises dramatically from the ground, evoking a sense of awe and spirituality. Its interior is adorned with striking stained glass and sculptures, creating a captivating visual experience.

Another notable landmark is the Palácio do Planalto, the official workplace of the President of Brazil. This sleek, white structure features Niemeyer's characteristic curved forms and clean lines, embodying the principles of modernist architecture. The Palácio da Alvorada, the President's residence, is equally impressive, with its minimalist design and stunning views of Lake Paranoá.

Brasília is also home to numerous other architectural marvels. The National Congress, composed of two towering domed structures, houses the Senate and Chamber of Deputies. The Itamaraty Palace, the headquarters of Brazil's Ministry of Foreign Affairs, showcases Niemeyer's signature style with its fluid lines and bold geometric shapes. The city's numerous residential buildings, known as superblocks, were designed to provide a harmonious living environment, combining functionality with aesthetic appeal.

The construction of Brasília was not without controversy. Critics argued that the rapid development of the city neglected the existing social and economic challenges faced by the country. The displacement of indigenous communities and rural populations raised concerns about the social impact of the project. However, supporters of Brasília emphasized its transformative potential, promoting economic growth, centralizing government functions, and fostering national unity.

Over the years, Brasília has evolved and grown, accommodating a population that exceeds three million people. Its modernist architecture and urban planning continue to be celebrated, earning recognition as a UNESCO World Heritage Site in 1987. The city has become a symbol of Brazilian modernism and an important cultural and political center.

Brasília's architectural legacy extends beyond its physical structures. It represents a vision of progress and a testament to the potential of human ingenuity and creativity. The birth of Brasília remains a significant milestone in Brazil's history, showcasing the country's commitment to embracing modernity, pushing boundaries, and embracing innovation in the pursuit of a brighter future.

# Military Dictatorship: Political Repression and the Struggle for Democracy

The period of the military dictatorship in Brazil, which lasted from 1964 to 1985, represents a challenging chapter in the nation's history. This era was characterized by political repression, curtailment of civil liberties, and a struggle for the restoration of democracy. Understanding the complexities and consequences of this period is crucial in comprehending Brazil's journey towards democratic governance.

The military dictatorship was initiated by a coup d'état on March 31, 1964, which overthrew the democratically elected government of President João Goulart. The coup was driven by a combination of factors, including concerns about Goulart's left-leaning policies, economic instability, and fears of communist influence. The military assumed power, establishing a junta that governed the country.

Under the military regime, Brazil experienced a profound consolidation of power in the hands of the armed forces. Institutional checks and balances were weakened, and democratic institutions were undermined. The regime imposed strict censorship, suppressing freedom of the press and limiting political expression. Political parties were banned, and dissenting voices were silenced.

During this period, the military government implemented a range of policies and practices to consolidate its control. These included arbitrary arrests, torture, and disappearances of individuals considered to be political opponents or threats to the regime. The National Security Law, enacted in 1969, granted broad powers to the military, allowing for the persecution of perceived subversives and dissenters.

Economically, the military regime pursued a policy of state-led development and modernization. The government implemented ambitious infrastructure projects, such as the construction of highways, dams, and industrial centers. This period also witnessed the expansion of industries, particularly in the energy and automotive sectors, as the government sought to boost economic growth and self-sufficiency.

The military regime's economic policies brought about a period of growth and stability, known as the "Brazilian Economic Miracle." However, these gains were accompanied by rising inequality and concentration of wealth, exacerbating social divisions within Brazilian society.

The military government faced resistance and opposition from various sectors of society. Students, intellectuals, labor unions, and religious organizations played crucial roles in challenging the authoritarian regime. Protests, strikes, and acts of civil disobedience became common forms of resistance against the dictatorship.

The 1970s marked a turning point in Brazil's struggle for democracy. The regime faced increasing criticism and international pressure due to its human rights abuses and political repression. The Catholic Church, through the Brazilian Bishops' Conference, emerged as a prominent voice for human rights and social justice, condemning the regime's actions and advocating for democratic reforms.

Gradually, the military regime began to lose its grip on power. In the late 1970s, a process of gradual political opening, known as "distensão," was initiated, allowing for limited political participation and the gradual restoration of civil liberties. The regime also faced economic challenges, including a debt crisis and inflation, which further weakened its authority.

In 1985, Brazil's military dictatorship finally came to an end. The country witnessed a peaceful transition to democracy with the election of civilian president José Sarney. This marked a significant milestone in Brazil's history, as it signaled the restoration of democratic governance and the reestablishment of fundamental rights and freedoms.

The legacy of the military dictatorship continues to shape Brazil's political and social landscape. The country has grappled with the need to address past human rights violations, provide accountability for the crimes committed during that period, and promote reconciliation among its citizens. The struggle for truth, justice, and memory remains ongoing, with initiatives such as the Truth Commission established to investigate and document human rights abuses.

The military dictatorship era serves as a reminder of the fragility of democracy and the importance of safeguarding democratic institutions. It highlights the resilience and determination of the Brazilian people in their fight for political freedom and the protection of human rights. The lessons learned from this period continue to inform Brazil's commitment to democratic governance, respect for human rights, and the pursuit of a more inclusive and just society.

# Brazilian Culture: Literature, Music, and Cinema

Brazilian culture is rich and diverse, reflecting the country's vibrant history, multicultural heritage, and creative spirit. From literature to music and cinema, Brazil has produced notable artists, works, and cultural movements that have captivated audiences both domestically and internationally.

Literature holds a significant place in Brazilian culture, with a long tradition of renowned writers and literary movements. One of the most influential figures in Brazilian literature is Machado de Assis, often regarded as Brazil's greatest writer. His works, such as "The Posthumous Memoirs of Brás Cubas" and "Dom Casmurro," explore themes of identity, society, and human nature with wit and depth.

Modernist literature emerged in the early 20th century, challenging traditional literary conventions and embracing new artistic expressions. The Modernist movement in Brazil, led by writers like Mário de Andrade and Oswald de Andrade, celebrated Brazilian identity, folklore, and regional diversity. Mário de Andrade's novel "Macunaíma" became a landmark work in Brazilian literature, blending elements of myth, satire, and cultural critique.

In the mid-20th century, a wave of regionalist literature emerged, highlighting the cultural, social, and historical aspects of different regions of Brazil. Writers like Graciliano Ramos and Jorge Amado portrayed the realities and complexities of life in the Northeast and the Northeastern cultural traditions, respectively, through their novels "Barren Lives" and "Gabriela, Clove and Cinnamon."

Brazilian music is renowned worldwide for its diversity and rhythmic richness. Samba, a genre that originated in Rio de Janeiro, is perhaps the most iconic Brazilian musical style. It emerged from Afro-Brazilian cultural influences and is characterized by lively percussion, melodic lines, and poetic lyrics. The music of legendary composers like Cartola, Noel Rosa, and Ary Barroso contributed to the development and popularization of samba.

Another prominent musical genre is bossa nova, which gained international recognition in the 1960s. Born in Rio de Janeiro, bossa nova combines samba rhythms with influences from jazz, creating a melodic and harmonically sophisticated style. The talents of composers like Antônio Carlos Jobim and João Gilberto, as well as the mesmerizing voice of singer Astrud Gilberto, helped popularize bossa nova worldwide.

Brazilian popular music also encompasses a wide range of styles and genres, including forró, frevo, axé, and funk carioca, among others. These genres showcase Brazil's regional diversity and cultural expressions, representing the rhythmic and melodic tapestry of the country.

Brazilian cinema has a long and storied history, marked by notable directors, acclaimed films, and international recognition. The Cinema Novo movement, emerging in the 1960s, represented a turning point in Brazilian cinema. Filmmakers like Glauber Rocha and Nelson Pereira dos Santos explored social issues, political commentary, and a distinct Brazilian identity through their works. Glauber Rocha's film "Black God, White Devil" and Nelson Pereira dos Santos's "Vidas Secas" are considered classics of Brazilian cinema.

The 1990s witnessed a resurgence in Brazilian cinema, with a new generation of filmmakers making their mark on the international stage. Films like "Central Station" directed by Walter Salles and "City of God" directed by Fernando Meirelles garnered critical acclaim and brought Brazilian cinema to the global spotlight.

Brazilian culture is also deeply connected to Carnival, an annual celebration known for its exuberant parades, vibrant costumes, and infectious music. Carnival showcases the diversity of Brazilian music, dance, and folklore, with samba schools competing to put on the most captivating performances. The Carnival of Rio de Janeiro, in particular, has become internationally renowned for its grandiosity and artistic excellence.

Beyond literature, music, and cinema, Brazilian culture encompasses a vast array of artistic expressions, including theater, visual arts, architecture, and culinary traditions. Artists like Tarsila do Amaral, Candido Portinari, and Oscar Niemeyer have left indelible marks on Brazilian art and architecture, capturing the essence of the country's landscapes, people, and cultural identity.

Brazilian culture continues to evolve and thrive, with new voices emerging and innovative expressions taking shape. It serves as a reflection of Brazil's diverse society, rich history, and the creative spirit of its people. The cultural achievements of Brazil have resonated globally, contributing to a greater understanding and appreciation of the country's artistic contributions and cultural heritage.

# Economic Miracle and Debt Crisis: Ups and Downs of Brazil's Economy

Brazil's economy has experienced significant ups and downs throughout its history, marked by periods of growth and prosperity as well as challenges and setbacks. Two notable phases in Brazil's economic trajectory are the "Economic Miracle" of the 1960s and 1970s and the subsequent debt crisis of the 1980s.

The Economic Miracle, also known as the "Brazilian Miracle," refers to a period of rapid economic growth that occurred from the late 1960s to the mid-1970s. During this time, Brazil experienced high rates of industrialization, urbanization, and modernization. The government implemented policies to promote economic development, attracting foreign investment and encouraging domestic industries.

One of the key drivers of the Economic Miracle was the expansion of the industrial sector. The government provided incentives for industrial growth, leading to the establishment of manufacturing plants, particularly in sectors such as automotive, steel, and petrochemicals. This industrial boom contributed to job creation, increased productivity, and a rise in living standards for many Brazilians.

The Economic Miracle also saw significant infrastructure development, with the construction of highways, hydroelectric dams, and other large-scale projects. These investments aimed to support industrial growth, improve transportation networks, and facilitate the movement of goods and people across the country.

During this period, Brazil experienced high rates of economic growth, often exceeding 10% per year. The Gross Domestic Product (GDP) expanded, and Brazil became the world's tenth-largest economy. This economic boom brought optimism and a sense of progress to the country, positioning Brazil as a rising global player.

However, the Economic Miracle also had its challenges and limitations. Economic growth was unevenly distributed, with wealth and opportunities concentrated in urban areas while rural poverty persisted. Income inequality widened, exacerbating social divisions within Brazilian society.

The subsequent debt crisis of the 1980s emerged as a result of macroeconomic imbalances and external factors. Brazil had accumulated substantial foreign debt during the Economic Miracle, mainly through borrowing from international financial institutions and commercial banks. A combination of factors, including high inflation, declining terms of trade, and global economic conditions, led to a situation where Brazil struggled to service its debt obligations.

The debt crisis had severe repercussions for Brazil's economy. The government faced challenges in managing its external debt and maintaining economic stability. Inflation soared, reaching hyperinflationary levels, which eroded the purchasing power of the population and created economic uncertainty.

To address the debt crisis and stabilize the economy, Brazil implemented a series of economic reforms and structural adjustment programs in the 1990s. These measures included fiscal austerity, privatization of state-owned enterprises, and the implementation of a new currency, the Real, to replace the hyperinflationary Cruzeiro.

Over time, Brazil's economy gradually recovered from the debt crisis. Macroeconomic stability was restored, and inflation was brought under control. The country experienced periods of moderate economic growth and made efforts to diversify its economy, reduce dependence on commodities, and attract foreign investment.

Despite these advancements, Brazil continues to face economic challenges, including persistent inequality, informal labor markets, and structural issues. The country's economy is influenced by global market trends, commodity prices, and internal factors such as governance, infrastructure, and education.

Brazil's economic trajectory underscores the complexity and volatility of global economic forces. The experiences of the Economic Miracle and the subsequent debt crisis serve as reminders of the need for sustainable and inclusive economic development. As Brazil navigates its economic path, policymakers strive to address the country's economic challenges and foster long-term stability, growth, and prosperity for all Brazilians.

# Environmental Awareness: Conservation Efforts and Challenges

Environmental awareness and conservation have become increasingly important in Brazil as the country grapples with the preservation of its diverse ecosystems and natural resources. Efforts to protect the environment have been driven by a recognition of the crucial role that nature plays in sustaining life, as well as the need to address pressing environmental challenges.

Brazil is home to the Amazon rainforest, the world's largest tropical rainforest, which is often referred to as the "lungs of the Earth." This vast and biodiverse ecosystem, along with other biomes such as the Pantanal wetlands and the Atlantic Forest, harbor unique flora and fauna, including endangered species. Protecting these ecosystems is crucial for global biodiversity conservation and climate regulation.

The Brazilian government has implemented various initiatives to promote environmental conservation. One of the key measures is the establishment of protected areas, such as national parks, biological reserves, and sustainable development reserves. These areas serve as havens for wildlife, protect indigenous territories, and preserve fragile ecosystems.

Efforts to combat deforestation and promote sustainable land use have also been a priority. The Brazilian Forest Code, enacted to regulate land use in the Amazon and other biomes, sets guidelines for forest preservation and requires landowners to maintain a certain percentage of their property as native vegetation. The government has also implemented monitoring systems, such as satellite-based deforestation detection, to enforce compliance and track changes in forest cover.

International cooperation has played a crucial role in supporting Brazil's environmental conservation efforts. Organizations such as the Amazon Environmental Research Institute (IPAM) and the Brazilian Biodiversity Fund (FUNBIO) have worked with local communities, government agencies, and international partners to develop sustainable practices, promote research, and support conservation projects.

However, Brazil also faces significant challenges in its environmental conservation efforts. Deforestation, illegal logging, and land encroachment continue to threaten the integrity of the country's forests. The expansion of agriculture, particularly cattle ranching and soybean production, has been a major driver of deforestation in the Amazon. Balancing the need for economic development with the imperative of environmental protection remains a delicate and complex task.

The preservation of Brazil's freshwater resources is another important aspect of environmental conservation. The country is home to an extensive network of rivers, including the Amazon and its tributaries, which provide critical water resources and support aquatic ecosystems. However, pollution, dam construction, and unsustainable water management practices pose challenges to the preservation of water quality and the protection of freshwater biodiversity.

Climate change presents another significant environmental challenge for Brazil. Rising temperatures, changing rainfall patterns, and increased frequency of extreme weather events threaten ecosystems, agricultural productivity, and vulnerable communities. Brazil has made commitments under international agreements, such as the Paris Agreement, to reduce greenhouse gas emissions, promote renewable energy sources, and adapt to the impacts of climate change.

Environmental awareness and activism have gained traction in Brazil, with civil society organizations, indigenous communities, and concerned citizens playing a crucial role in advocating for conservation and sustainable development. The environmental movement has successfully raised awareness about the importance of protecting natural resources and has influenced public policies and corporate practices.

Education and public engagement are key to fostering a culture of environmental stewardship. Schools, universities, and educational institutions play a vital role in promoting environmental education, raising awareness about conservation issues, and instilling a sense of responsibility toward the environment in future generations.

In conclusion, environmental awareness and conservation efforts have become increasingly prominent in Brazil. While the country faces significant challenges in preserving its ecosystems and natural resources, there is a growing recognition of the importance of environmental stewardship. Continued efforts to address deforestation, promote sustainable land use, protect freshwater resources, mitigate climate change, and engage the public are essential for ensuring the long-term sustainability and well-being of Brazil's environment and its people.

# Pantanal: A Wetland Paradise

The Pantanal is a vast wetland located primarily in western Brazil, but also extending into Bolivia and Paraguay. It is one of the world's largest freshwater wetland ecosystems and is renowned for its remarkable biodiversity and natural beauty. The Pantanal is often referred to as a "wetland paradise" due to its unique characteristics and ecological significance.

Spanning an area of approximately 150,000 square kilometers, the Pantanal is home to an incredible diversity of flora and fauna. It is estimated that the region harbors over 4,700 species of plants, 1,000 species of birds, 300 species of fish, 124 species of mammals, and countless invertebrates. This biodiversity has earned the Pantanal recognition as a UNESCO World Heritage Site and a Ramsar Wetland of International Importance.

The Pantanal's landscape is characterized by a mosaic of flooded plains, seasonally inundated areas, lagoons, and rivers. The region experiences distinct wet and dry seasons, with the wet season occurring from November to March and the dry season from April to October. During the wet season, rainfall fills the Pantanal's rivers and tributaries, transforming the landscape into a vast aquatic expanse.

The flooding of the Pantanal creates a dynamic ecosystem that supports an abundance of life. It provides critical habitats for numerous species, including caimans, capybaras, giant otters, jaguars, anacondas, and a plethora of bird species. The wetland serves as a breeding ground and feeding area for migratory birds, attracting birdwatchers and nature enthusiasts from around the world.

The Pantanal's rich aquatic environment sustains an extraordinary diversity of fish species, which, in turn, support the wetland's predators, such as the elusive and majestic jaguar. This apex predator is known to roam the Pantanal's marshes and riverbanks, drawing wildlife enthusiasts who hope to catch a glimpse of this elusive feline in its natural habitat.

Indigenous communities have long inhabited the Pantanal and have developed a deep connection with its natural resources. They have relied on traditional knowledge and sustainable practices to coexist harmoniously with the wetland's ecosystems. Their cultural heritage and traditional lifestyles contribute to the richness and cultural significance of the Pantanal.

The Pantanal also plays a vital ecological role beyond its borders. It serves as a natural water regulator, absorbing and gradually releasing water into the Paraguay River Basin, thus mitigating the impact of floods and droughts. The wetland acts as a natural filter, purifying water and contributing to the overall water quality of the region.

Tourism has emerged as an important economic activity in the Pantanal, providing opportunities for visitors to explore and appreciate the wetland's natural wonders. Responsible ecotourism practices aim to minimize environmental impact and promote sustainable development, ensuring the long-term preservation of the Pantanal's fragile ecosystems.

Conservation efforts in the Pantanal are crucial to safeguard its biodiversity and ecological balance. Various organizations, research institutions, and governmental agencies collaborate to protect the wetland, monitor wildlife populations, and address environmental threats.

These threats include deforestation, illegal fishing, pollution, and the potential impacts of climate change.

As with any ecosystem, the Pantanal faces challenges in maintaining its delicate balance. Balancing conservation with economic development, promoting sustainable land use practices, and addressing environmental pressures are ongoing endeavors. Collaboration between stakeholders, including local communities, governments, and conservation organizations, remains essential to the long-term preservation of this unique wetland paradise.

In conclusion, the Pantanal stands as a wetland paradise of remarkable beauty, incredible biodiversity, and ecological significance. Its vast flooded plains, diverse wildlife, and cultural heritage make it a cherished natural gem. Protecting and preserving the Pantanal ensures the continued existence of this remarkable ecosystem for future generations to appreciate and cherish.

# Brazilian Coastline: Marine Life and Coral Reefs

Brazil is blessed with a vast and diverse coastline that stretches for approximately 7,400 kilometers along the Atlantic Ocean. This extensive coastal stretch encompasses a range of marine ecosystems, including vibrant coral reefs, rich coastal mangroves, and diverse marine life. The Brazilian coastline holds immense ecological value and provides a habitat for a wide array of marine species.

One of the most remarkable features of the Brazilian coastline is its coral reefs. These delicate and biodiverse ecosystems play a vital role in marine biodiversity and provide crucial habitats for numerous species. The reefs are home to an impressive variety of coral species, such as brain corals, staghorn corals, and pillar corals, which form intricate structures that support a complex web of marine life.

The Abrolhos Bank, located off the coast of Bahia, is one of the most important and well-known coral reef systems in Brazil. It is home to the largest concentration of marine biodiversity in the South Atlantic Ocean and serves as a breeding ground and nursery for various fish species, sea turtles, and marine mammals. The Abrolhos Marine National Park was established to protect this unique ecosystem and preserve its ecological integrity.

The Brazilian coastline also supports a diverse range of marine species beyond coral reefs. Its waters are home to numerous fish species, including colorful tropical fish, groupers, snappers, and sardines, among others. The coastline provides feeding grounds and migration routes for marine mammals, such as dolphins, whales, and manatees, which can be observed in different regions along the coast.

Mangroves, found in many coastal areas, are another essential feature of the Brazilian coastline. These unique ecosystems thrive in the brackish waters where rivers meet the sea, serving as a buffer between land and ocean. Mangroves provide critical nursery areas for juvenile fish and other marine organisms, and their dense root systems help stabilize coastlines, protect against erosion, and filter pollutants from runoff.

The Brazilian coastline also boasts a range of marine protected areas and conservation initiatives aimed at preserving its fragile ecosystems. These include national parks, marine reserves, and sustainable fishing practices that promote responsible resource management and support the long-term sustainability of marine resources.

Despite these conservation efforts, the Brazilian coastline faces various environmental challenges. Overfishing, pollution from urban areas and industrial activities, habitat degradation, and climate change impact the health and resilience of marine ecosystems. Rising sea temperatures, ocean acidification, and extreme weather events can all have detrimental effects on coral reefs and marine life.

To address these challenges, Brazil has implemented measures to promote marine conservation and sustainable practices. The country has adopted policies and regulations to protect endangered species, control fishing activities, and reduce pollution in coastal areas. Efforts are underway to increase public awareness of the importance of marine conservation and the need to protect the fragile ecosystems along the Brazilian coastline.

Scientific research and monitoring play a crucial role in understanding and managing the marine environments along the Brazilian coastline. Research institutions, universities, and governmental agencies collaborate to study marine biodiversity, assess the health of coral reefs, monitor fish populations, and develop strategies for effective conservation and sustainable management.

The Brazilian coastline is a valuable natural asset that contributes to the country's cultural heritage, economic activities, and ecological balance. It serves as a reminder of the interconnectedness of land and sea and the need to protect and preserve these fragile ecosystems for future generations. The conservation of marine life and coral reefs along the Brazilian coastline requires ongoing efforts, collaboration, and a commitment to sustainable practices to ensure the long-term health and vitality of these precious marine ecosystems.

# Atlantic Forest: Biodiversity and Preservation Efforts

The Atlantic Forest, also known as the Mata Atlântica, is a vast and biodiverse tropical forest ecosystem that once stretched along the eastern coast of Brazil, extending into parts of Argentina and Paraguay. Today, remnants of this magnificent forest remain, showcasing its incredible biodiversity and serving as a reminder of the urgent need for conservation and preservation efforts.

The Atlantic Forest is recognized as one of the world's most important biodiversity hotspots. It is estimated to contain around 20,000 plant species, of which approximately 8,000 are endemic, meaning they are found nowhere else in the world. The forest supports an impressive variety of wildlife, including rare and endangered species such as the golden lion tamarin, the jaguar, the maned sloth, and the harpy eagle.

The forest's remarkable biodiversity is a result of its diverse topography and range of microclimates. From coastal areas to mountainous regions, the Atlantic Forest encompasses a range of ecosystems, including dense forests, montane forests, mangroves, and grasslands. This variation in habitats contributes to the high level of species richness and endemism found within the forest.

The Atlantic Forest has faced significant threats over the years, primarily due to human activities. Extensive deforestation for agriculture, urbanization, and logging has resulted in the loss of a substantial portion of the original forest cover. It is estimated that less than 10% of the original Atlantic Forest remains today, making it one of the most endangered and fragmented ecosystems on the planet.

Recognizing the importance of preserving the remaining fragments, conservation organizations, government agencies, and local communities have made significant efforts to protect and restore the Atlantic Forest. Numerous protected areas have been established throughout the region, including national parks, biological reserves, and private nature reserves. These areas provide refuge for threatened species and contribute to the connectivity and restoration of the forest ecosystem.

Restoration initiatives have also been vital in reclaiming degraded areas and reconnecting fragmented forest patches. Reforestation programs, involving the planting of native tree species, help to restore ecological corridors and enhance habitat connectivity for wildlife. These efforts contribute to the preservation of the forest's biodiversity and ecosystem services.

The Atlantic Forest is not only essential for its biodiversity but also plays a critical role in providing ecosystem services. The forest helps regulate water flow, contributing to the stability of watersheds and water availability for surrounding communities. It also supports soil conservation, carbon sequestration, and climate regulation, making it a significant ally in the fight against climate change.

Sustainable land-use practices and community engagement are crucial components of preserving the Atlantic Forest. Collaborative initiatives involving local communities, landowners, and conservation organizations aim to promote sustainable agriculture, agroforestry, and the development of eco-tourism as alternative sources of income. These approaches provide economic incentives for local communities to protect the forest while ensuring the long-term sustainability of the ecosystem.

Scientific research and monitoring play a vital role in understanding the Atlantic Forest's biodiversity, ecology, and the impacts of human activities. Researchers and institutions collaborate to study species distribution, monitor ecosystem health, and assess the effectiveness of conservation measures. This knowledge informs decision-making processes and helps shape effective conservation strategies.

The preservation of the Atlantic Forest is an ongoing endeavor that requires long-term commitment, cooperation, and awareness. Efforts to combat deforestation, promote sustainable land-use practices, and engage local communities in conservation initiatives are essential. Public education and awareness campaigns play a crucial role in fostering a sense of stewardship and inspiring action to protect this invaluable ecosystem.

The Atlantic Forest stands as a testament to Brazil's natural heritage and holds immense ecological, cultural, and scientific value. Its preservation not only benefits the region but also contributes to global efforts in biodiversity conservation and sustainable development. Through continued conservation efforts, the hope is to safeguard the Atlantic Forest's biodiversity and ensure its survival for generations to come.

# The Marvels of Brazilian Diving: Exploring the Underwater World

Brazil offers diving enthusiasts an incredible array of underwater wonders to explore. From vibrant coral reefs and diverse marine life to unique geological formations and historic shipwrecks, the country's coastal and marine environments present a captivating world beneath the waves.

One of the most renowned diving destinations in Brazil is Fernando de Noronha, a remote archipelago located off the northeastern coast. Its crystal-clear waters and abundant marine life make it a paradise for divers. The archipelago is home to stunning coral reefs teeming with colorful fish, turtles, dolphins, and even the occasional encounter with gentle reef sharks. Exploring the underwater landscape of Fernando de Noronha is a breathtaking experience.

The Abrolhos Marine National Park, off the coast of Bahia, is another remarkable diving destination. Its coral reefs, particularly the Parcel dos Abrolhos reef, are considered one of the most important coral ecosystems in the South Atlantic. Divers can witness the beauty of hard and soft corals, encounter schools of tropical fish, and marvel at the sight of humpback whales during their breeding season.

In addition to coral reefs, Brazil's coastline is dotted with intriguing geological formations that attract divers from around the world. The natural arches and caverns of Arraial do Cabo, located in Rio de Janeiro state, offer a unique underwater landscape to explore. These formations, sculpted by the forces of nature, create stunning underwater corridors and swim-throughs, providing a sense of adventure and awe for divers.

For those interested in diving alongside historical relics, the coast of Brazil also offers opportunities to explore shipwrecks. The rich maritime history of the region has left behind a number of intriguing wrecks that have become fascinating underwater habitats. The "Vapor Bahia," a steamship that sank in 1910 off the coast of São Paulo, is one such example. Diving enthusiasts can explore the remnants of the ship, witnessing the transformation of the vessel into an artificial reef, attracting a variety of marine life.

Brazil's marine biodiversity is awe-inspiring, with an incredible variety of fish, invertebrates, and other marine species. Divers may encounter species such as angelfish, parrotfish, moray eels, rays, and even the majestic seahorse. The country's warm waters and diverse ecosystems provide habitats for an abundance of marine life, making every dive a unique and exciting experience.

To ensure the preservation of these underwater marvels, conservation efforts are crucial. Marine protected areas, such as national parks and marine reserves, play a vital role in safeguarding the health and integrity of the marine ecosystems. These protected areas not only offer refuge for marine life but also provide opportunities for scientific research and education.

Diving in Brazil is regulated by environmental laws and guidelines to ensure the sustainable use of marine resources and minimize environmental impact. Divers are encouraged to follow responsible diving practices, such as avoiding contact with delicate coral reefs, not disturbing marine life, and properly disposing of any waste.

Diving in Brazil is a captivating experience that allows individuals to connect with the beauty and diversity of the underwater world. Whether exploring coral reefs, encountering marine life, or discovering historic shipwrecks, divers have the opportunity to witness firsthand the wonders that lie beneath the surface of Brazil's coastal waters. The exploration of the underwater world not only offers a sense of adventure and discovery but also fosters appreciation for the importance of marine conservation and the need to protect these fragile ecosystems for future generations to enjoy.

# Rio de Janeiro: The Marvelous City

Rio de Janeiro, often referred to as the "Marvelous City," is a vibrant and iconic metropolis located in southeastern Brazil. Known for its stunning landscapes, rich cultural heritage, and lively atmosphere, Rio de Janeiro captivates visitors from around the world with its unique blend of natural beauty and urban charm.

One of Rio de Janeiro's most famous landmarks is the majestic Christ the Redeemer statue, which stands atop the Corcovado Mountain, offering panoramic views of the city. This iconic symbol of Brazil welcomes millions of visitors each year, who come to marvel at its grandeur and admire the breathtaking vistas of Rio's stunning coastline, lush forests, and vibrant neighborhoods.

Rio de Janeiro is blessed with beautiful beaches that have become synonymous with the city's laid-back lifestyle and love for outdoor activities. Copacabana Beach, with its iconic black and white mosaic promenade, stretches for miles, offering a lively atmosphere where locals and tourists gather to sunbathe, play beach volleyball, and enjoy the ocean breeze. Ipanema Beach, known for its golden sands and breathtaking sunsets, has been immortalized in songs and stories, capturing the imagination of people worldwide.

The city's geography is dominated by the Tijuca National Park, the largest urban forest in the world. This tropical forest covers an area of over 3,000 hectares and provides a lush green sanctuary within the bustling cityscape. Tijuca Forest offers numerous trails for hiking, cascading waterfalls, and hidden viewpoints that allow visitors to immerse themselves in nature and escape the urban hustle and bustle.

Cultural diversity is at the heart of Rio de Janeiro's identity. The city is a melting pot of different ethnicities, traditions, and artistic expressions. It is home to the annual Carnival, a world-renowned festival that celebrates Brazilian culture with vibrant parades, samba music, and extravagant costumes. During this festive season, Rio comes alive with energy and excitement, as locals and visitors revel in the joyful atmosphere that permeates the streets.

The neighborhoods of Rio de Janeiro each have their distinct character and charm. The historic district of Santa Teresa, with its colonial architecture and winding streets, offers a bohemian atmosphere and is a haven for artists and intellectuals. The modern neighborhood of Barra da Tijuca, with its high-rise buildings and expansive malls, represents Rio's cosmopolitan side and is a popular destination for shopping and entertainment.

Sports hold a special place in the heart of Cariocas, the residents of Rio de Janeiro. The city has hosted numerous international sporting events, including the FIFA World Cup and the Olympic Games. The Maracanã Stadium, one of the world's most famous football stadiums, has witnessed legendary matches and is a symbol of the city's passion for the beautiful game.

Rio de Janeiro's culinary scene is as diverse as its population. From traditional Brazilian dishes to international cuisines, the city offers a gastronomic adventure for food enthusiasts. Local specialties such as feijoada (a hearty black bean stew with meat) and pão de queijo (cheese bread) delight the taste buds, while churrascarias (Brazilian BBQ restaurants) offer a carnivorous feast.

The city's cultural institutions, such as the Rio de Janeiro Museum of Art (MAR) and the National Museum of Fine Arts, showcase a wealth of artistic masterpieces, both Brazilian and international. The vibrant music scene of Rio de Janeiro encompasses genres such as bossa nova, samba, and funk carioca, and the city's nightlife offers a wide range of entertainment options, from samba clubs to trendy bars and music venues.

Safety is an important consideration when visiting Rio de Janeiro. While the city has made efforts to improve security and provide a safe environment for residents and visitors, it is advisable to take necessary precautions, such as avoiding certain areas at night and being aware of your surroundings.

In conclusion, Rio de Janeiro is a city that captivates with its natural beauty, cultural richness, and vibrant spirit. From its iconic landmarks to its stunning beaches, from its diverse neighborhoods to its lively festivals, Rio de Janeiro offers a unique and unforgettable experience for those who seek to immerse themselves in the marvels of this captivating city.

# Salvador: Afro-Brazilian Culture and Historic Center

Salvador, the capital of the state of Bahia in northeastern Brazil, is a city rich in Afro-Brazilian culture and history. Known for its vibrant music, dance, cuisine, and stunning architecture, Salvador offers visitors a unique glimpse into the fusion of African, European, and Indigenous influences that have shaped its identity over the centuries.

The historic center of Salvador, known as the Pelourinho, is a UNESCO World Heritage site and a testament to the city's colonial past. Its cobblestone streets, colorful colonial buildings, and ornate churches create an enchanting atmosphere that transports visitors back in time. The Pelourinho is home to several significant landmarks, including the São Francisco Church, with its lavish gold-covered interior, and the Lacerda Elevator, which provides panoramic views of the city.

One of the defining aspects of Salvador is its strong Afro-Brazilian heritage. The city is considered the heart of Afro-Brazilian culture, where traditions rooted in African customs and spirituality thrive. The Candomblé religion, brought to Brazil by enslaved Africans, plays a significant role in the cultural fabric of Salvador. Candomblé ceremonies, characterized by music, dance, and spiritual rituals, can be witnessed in various terreiros (religious houses) throughout the city.

Music and dance are integral to Salvador's identity, and the rhythms of Afro-Brazilian music resonate through its streets. The energetic beats of samba-reggae, axé, and capoeira echo throughout the city, inviting locals and visitors to dance and celebrate. The Carnival of Salvador, often considered one of the largest street parties in the world, showcases the city's vibrant music and dance culture, with blocos (parade groups) and trios elétricos (music trucks) filling the streets with joyful revelry.

The African influence is also evident in Salvador's culinary traditions. The city's cuisine is a fusion of African, Indigenous, and Portuguese flavors, resulting in a unique gastronomic experience. Acarajé, a deep-fried black-eyed pea fritter filled with shrimp, vatapá (a rich and spicy seafood stew), and moqueca (a flavorful fish stew) are just a few examples of the delicious Afro-Brazilian dishes that can be savored in Salvador.

Salvador's strong African heritage is also reflected in its population, with a significant Afro-Brazilian majority. The city's demographics and social fabric are shaped by the legacy of slavery and the resilience of the African diaspora. Cultural expressions such as capoeira, a martial art form with roots in African dance and self-defense, are not only celebrated but also serve as a reminder of the struggle and resilience of Afro-Brazilian communities.

Beyond its cultural richness, Salvador boasts stunning natural beauty. Its coastline stretches for miles, offering picturesque beaches, such as Porto da Barra and Farol da Barra, where locals and visitors gather to relax, swim, and soak up the sun. The nearby islands of Itaparica and Morro de São Paulo provide idyllic retreats with crystal-clear waters and pristine sandy beaches.

As with any city, Salvador faces challenges, including poverty, inequality, and urban violence. However, efforts are being made to address these issues and promote social inclusion and economic development. Community-based initiatives, cultural preservation projects, and investments in infrastructure contribute to the ongoing revitalization of Salvador and the empowerment of its communities.

Salvador is a city that invites exploration and celebration of its Afro-Brazilian heritage. It is a place where history, culture, music, and cuisine intertwine to create a vibrant tapestry of experiences. The city's Afro-Brazilian roots provide a unique lens through which to appreciate the diversity and richness of Brazil's cultural landscape, making Salvador an essential destination for those seeking a deeper understanding of the country's complex history and heritage.

# Brasília: Modernist Architecture and Political Hub

Brasília, the capital of Brazil, stands as a testament to modernist architecture and urban planning. Designed by renowned architect Oscar Niemeyer and urban planner Lúcio Costa, the city's layout and buildings reflect a vision of progress, functionality, and efficiency. With its distinctive architectural style and status as the seat of Brazil's political power, Brasília has become an iconic symbol of the country's modern identity.

The construction of Brasília began in the late 1950s, with the intention of moving the capital from Rio de Janeiro to a more central location. The site chosen for the new capital was a vast, undeveloped area in the Brazilian interior known as the Planalto Central. Lúcio Costa envisioned a city divided into functional sectors, with each area dedicated to specific functions such as government, residential, commercial, and recreational.

The architectural centerpiece of Brasília is the National Congress building. Designed by Oscar Niemeyer, the building consists of two distinct structures: the Senate and the Chamber of Deputies. The futuristic design of the Congress building features sweeping curves, glass facades, and large open spaces, symbolizing transparency and democracy.

Another iconic structure in Brasília is the Cathedral of Brasília, also designed by Niemeyer. The cathedral's unique design resembles a crown of thorns, with 16 curved concrete columns that reach toward the sky. Inside, the natural light filtering through the stained glass creates a serene and ethereal atmosphere.

The city's urban layout is characterized by its rigid, geometric design. The central axis, known as the Eixo Monumental, is a long boulevard flanked by monumental buildings and landmarks. At the heart of the Eixo Monumental is the Praça dos Três Poderes (Three Powers Plaza), where the National Congress, the Presidential Palace (Palácio da Alvorada), and the Supreme Federal Court are located.

Brasília's residential areas are organized into superblocks, which consist of apartment buildings, green spaces, and shared facilities such as schools and shopping centers. The superblock concept aimed to promote community living and foster a sense of belonging among residents. However, this model has also been subject to criticism for its perceived lack of social integration and walkability.

As the political center of Brazil, Brasília is home to various government institutions, ministries, and foreign embassies. The Presidential Palace, designed by Oscar Niemeyer, serves as the official residence of the President of Brazil. The city also houses the headquarters of the Supreme Federal Court, the National Library, and numerous other government buildings.

Brasília's status as the capital and its modernist architecture have made it a cultural and tourist destination. The city attracts visitors who are interested in exploring its architectural landmarks, visiting museums, and experiencing its unique urban environment. The Brasília National Museum showcases Brazil's cultural and historical heritage, while the Juscelino Kubitschek Memorial provides insights into the city's creation and development.

While Brasília embodies the aspirations of Brazil's modern era, it has not been without its challenges. The city's construction involved the displacement of indigenous communities and the disruption of local ecosystems. Additionally, the perceived social isolation and high cost of living in Brasília have been subjects of criticism and debate.

Nevertheless, Brasília remains an important symbol of Brazil's ambition and progress. Its modernist architecture and urban design continue to inspire architects and urban planners around the world. The city's role as the political hub of Brazil ensures its significance as a center of power and decision-making.

In conclusion, Brasília stands as a remarkable testament to modernist architecture and urban planning. Its visionary design, iconic buildings, and central role in Brazil's political landscape make it a city of great importance and intrigue. Whether admired for its architectural achievements, explored for its cultural offerings, or studied for its unique urban layout, Brasília is an enduring symbol of Brazil's modern aspirations.

# São Paulo: The Financial and Cultural Heart of Brazil

São Paulo, the largest city in Brazil and one of the largest in the world, serves as the financial and cultural heart of the country. With its bustling streets, towering skyscrapers, diverse population, and vibrant cultural scene, São Paulo embodies the dynamic and cosmopolitan spirit of Brazil.

The city's economic significance is undeniable. São Paulo is the financial hub of Brazil, hosting the headquarters of numerous national and international banks, financial institutions, and multinational corporations. It is a city of commerce and industry, attracting business professionals and entrepreneurs from all over the world. The São Paulo Stock Exchange, known as B3 (Bolsa de Valores, Mercadorias e Futuros), is a major player in Latin American financial markets.

São Paulo's economy is diversified, with sectors such as finance, manufacturing, technology, and services playing significant roles. The city is particularly renowned for its fashion industry, hosting São Paulo Fashion Week, one of the most prominent fashion events in the world. Additionally, São Paulo is a major center for the automotive industry, hosting the headquarters of several automobile manufacturers and playing a crucial role in Brazil's automotive production.

Beyond its economic prowess, São Paulo is a cultural powerhouse. The city boasts a vibrant arts and entertainment scene, with numerous theaters, art galleries, music venues, and museums. The São Paulo Museum of

Art (MASP) is one of the city's most iconic cultural institutions, housing an extensive collection of European and Brazilian artworks. The Pinacoteca do Estado and the Museum of Contemporary Art (MAC) are also highly regarded, showcasing a range of artistic expressions.

São Paulo is celebrated for its diverse culinary landscape. The city offers a cornucopia of flavors, with countless restaurants, cafes, and food markets representing cuisines from around the world. The influence of São Paulo's immigrant populations is evident in its culinary offerings, with Italian, Japanese, Lebanese, and Portuguese cuisines among the city's highlights. Street food culture thrives in São Paulo, with bustling food markets like the Mercado Municipal attracting food enthusiasts seeking traditional Brazilian delicacies.

The city's architecture is a fascinating blend of old and new. Historic buildings and neighborhoods such as the Pátio do Colégio and the Paulista Avenue showcase São Paulo's colonial and early 20th-century architectural heritage. In contrast, modernist landmarks like the Copan Building, designed by Oscar Niemeyer, and the São Paulo Museum of Art represent the city's contemporary architectural achievements. São Paulo's skyline is dominated by skyscrapers, reflecting its status as a global metropolis.

São Paulo's population is incredibly diverse, with people from all walks of life and various cultural backgrounds calling the city home. The influence of immigration is deeply ingrained in São Paulo's identity, with sizable communities of Italian, Japanese, Lebanese, and Portuguese descent, among others. This cultural diversity is reflected in the city's vibrant neighborhoods, each with its unique character and atmosphere.

The city's public transportation system is extensive, with a network of buses, trains, and the São Paulo Metro facilitating the movement of millions of people daily. São Paulo faces challenges related to traffic congestion and urban sprawl, but ongoing infrastructure projects and urban planning initiatives aim to improve mobility and enhance the quality of life for its residents.

São Paulo's energy is palpable, with a multitude of cultural events and festivals happening year-round. The city hosts the São Paulo International Film Festival, one of the largest film festivals in Latin America, attracting renowned filmmakers and cinephiles from around the world. The São Paulo Carnival, although not as famous as its counterpart in Rio de Janeiro, offers vibrant parades, street parties, and samba performances that celebrate Brazil's rich cultural heritage.

In conclusion, São Paulo stands as a testament to Brazil's economic prowess, cultural diversity, and urban vibrancy. It is a city of opportunities, where finance and commerce intersect with art, culture, and culinary delights. São Paulo's global influence and multifaceted character make it a captivating destination for those seeking a vibrant and cosmopolitan experience in the heart of Brazil.

# The Amazon River and Manaus: Gateway to the Rainforest

The Amazon River is one of the world's most iconic waterways, winding its way through the heart of the Amazon rainforest in South America. Spanning over 6,400 kilometers (4,000 miles), it is the largest river in terms of volume and carries more water than any other river on Earth. Its immense size, rich biodiversity, and cultural significance make it a fascinating and integral part of the Amazon region.

Originating in the Peruvian Andes, the Amazon River flows eastward across Brazil, passing through Colombia and Peru along the way. It eventually empties into the Atlantic Ocean, creating a vast estuary where freshwater mixes with the saltwater of the ocean. The river's extensive basin, known as the Amazon Basin, covers an area of approximately 7 million square kilometers (2.7 million square miles) and spans multiple countries.

The Amazon River and its tributaries are lifelines for both the wildlife and the human communities that inhabit the region. The river sustains an astonishing array of plant and animal species, many of which are found nowhere else on Earth. The Amazon rainforest, often referred to as the "lungs of the planet," plays a vital role in regulating the global climate and is home to an estimated 10% of the world's known species.

Manaus, the capital of the Brazilian state of Amazonas, serves as a gateway to the Amazon rainforest and is a significant port city along the Amazon River. Nestled deep in the heart of the rainforest, Manaus is a vibrant urban center that blends modernity with the natural wonders of the surrounding environment. The city's unique location offers visitors access to the diverse ecosystems, indigenous cultures, and captivating wildlife that characterize the Amazon region.

Manaus rose to prominence during the late 19th century due to the rubber boom, a period when rubber production and trade thrived in the Amazon Basin. The wealth generated by the rubber industry led to the construction of opulent buildings and the development of an elaborate urban infrastructure in the city. The iconic Teatro Amazonas, a magnificent opera house built in the heart of Manaus, stands as a testament to the city's prosperous past.

Today, Manaus is a bustling metropolis that serves as a hub for both tourists and researchers interested in exploring the wonders of the Amazon rainforest. The city offers a range of accommodations, from luxury hotels to eco-lodges, providing visitors with comfortable bases from which to embark on their Amazonian adventures. Guided tours and river cruises offer opportunities to explore the rainforest's diverse ecosystems, encounter indigenous communities, and observe the region's unique flora and fauna.

The Amazon River itself provides a means of transportation and sustenance for the communities that live along its banks. Riverine populations rely on the river for fishing, agriculture, and transportation, utilizing small boats and canoes as their primary mode of travel. Indigenous communities, with their deep-rooted connections to the land and the river, offer visitors a chance to learn about their traditional ways of life and their profound knowledge of the rainforest ecosystem.

In recent years, the Amazon region has faced various challenges, including deforestation, illegal logging, and the encroachment of human activities. These issues have raised concerns about the conservation of this vital ecosystem and the protection of indigenous cultures. Efforts are being made by local and international organizations, governments, and indigenous communities to promote sustainable practices, support conservation initiatives, and raise awareness about the importance of preserving the Amazon rainforest.

Visiting the Amazon River and Manaus offers a unique opportunity to witness the awe-inspiring beauty of the rainforest and gain a deeper appreciation for its ecological significance. It is a chance to immerse oneself in the natural wonders of the region, learn from the wisdom of indigenous cultures, and contribute to the conservation efforts that aim to safeguard this invaluable ecosystem for future generations.

In conclusion, the Amazon River and Manaus are gateways to the awe-inspiring Amazon rainforest. The river's grandeur and the city's position in the heart of the rainforest provide an unparalleled opportunity to explore the natural wonders, cultural richness, and ecological significance of this remarkable region. The Amazon River and Manaus beckon adventurers, nature enthusiasts, and cultural explorers to embrace the beauty and diversity that define the Amazonian experience.

# Iguazu Falls: Nature's Spectacular Display

Iguazu Falls, located on the border between Brazil and Argentina, is one of the most awe-inspiring natural wonders in the world. With its thunderous cascades, breathtaking vistas, and lush surroundings, it is a testament to the raw power and beauty of nature.

Spanning nearly 2.7 kilometers (1.7 miles) in width and consisting of approximately 275 individual falls, Iguazu Falls is one of the largest waterfall systems globally. It is formed by the Iguazu River as it plunges into a series of narrow basaltic gorges, creating an impressive display of cascades, mist, and rainbows.

The falls are surrounded by dense subtropical rainforest, known as the Iguazu National Park on the Argentine side and the Iguaçu National Park on the Brazilian side. These protected areas serve as havens for a wide array of flora and fauna, including jaguars, toucans, butterflies, and vibrant orchids. The parks are recognized as UNESCO World Heritage sites, honoring the natural and cultural significance of the region.

One of the most iconic features of Iguazu Falls is the Devil's Throat, or Garganta del Diablo in Spanish. This U-shaped waterfall measures approximately 82 meters (269 feet) in height and 150 meters (492 feet) in width. Standing at the edge of the platform overlooking the Devil's Throat, visitors are enveloped by the deafening roar of water as it plunges into the abyss below, creating a truly awe-inspiring experience.

The falls can be explored from both the Brazilian and Argentine sides, each offering a unique perspective and different vantage points. On the Brazilian side, visitors can walk along a series of well-maintained trails that provide panoramic views of the falls. The highlight is the walkway leading to the base of the Devil's Throat, where the immense power and intensity of the waterfall can be felt up close.

The Argentine side offers a more immersive experience, with a network of trails and walkways that take visitors through the lush rainforest and bring them closer to the individual falls. The Lower Circuit trail provides access to the base of some of the falls, allowing for a more intimate and wet encounter with the cascading waters. The Upper Circuit offers breathtaking views from elevated walkways, revealing the sheer magnitude and grandeur of the falls.

Boat tours are also available for those seeking a more adventurous experience. These excursions take visitors on thrilling rides along the river, bringing them face-to-face with the powerful spray of the falls. It's an exhilarating way to appreciate the sheer force and magnificence of Iguazu Falls.

Beyond the falls themselves, the surrounding national parks offer a range of activities and opportunities to explore the natural wonders of the region. Hiking trails wind through the rainforest, allowing visitors to discover the rich biodiversity and observe the unique flora and fauna that thrive in this environment. Birdwatching enthusiasts will be delighted by the variety of colorful avian species that inhabit the area.

The cultural heritage of the indigenous Guarani people is also an integral part of the Iguazu Falls experience. The Guarani have a deep spiritual connection to the falls, considering them sacred and imbued with mystical powers. Cultural encounters and guided tours provide insight into the Guarani's traditions, beliefs, and sustainable way of life.

Iguazu Falls is a remarkable testament to the power and grandeur of nature. Its magnificent waterfalls, surrounded by pristine rainforest and abundant wildlife, create an unforgettable sensory experience. The thundering sound of water, the mist that envelops the air, and the vibrant rainbows that emerge from the spray all contribute to the awe-inspiring spectacle that is Iguazu Falls.

In conclusion, Iguazu Falls stands as a testament to the remarkable beauty and power of nature. Its awe-inspiring waterfalls, encompassed by lush rainforest and teeming with biodiversity, create a truly unforgettable experience. Whether marveling at the panoramic views, walking along the trails, or embarking on an adventurous boat tour, visitors are sure to be captivated by the splendor of Iguazu Falls.

# Ouro Preto: Colonial Splendor in Minas Gerais

Ouro Preto, located in the state of Minas Gerais, Brazil, is a captivating city that showcases the colonial splendor of the country's past. With its well-preserved historic center, opulent churches, and rich cultural heritage, Ouro Preto offers visitors a glimpse into Brazil's colonial era and the wealth derived from the region's gold mines.

The city's history dates back to the late 17th century when gold was discovered in the surrounding hills and valleys. The newfound wealth attracted thousands of fortune seekers from all corners of Brazil and beyond, transforming the region into a bustling center of gold mining and trade. Ouro Preto, which translates to "Black Gold," derived its name from the precious metal that fueled its prosperity.

Ouro Preto's historic center is a UNESCO World Heritage site, recognized for its outstanding architectural and cultural value. The cobblestone streets, narrow alleys, and well-preserved colonial buildings transport visitors back in time, evoking the grandeur and opulence of the past. The city's architectural style is predominantly Baroque, characterized by intricate ornamentation, elaborate facades, and richly decorated interiors.

The churches of Ouro Preto stand as iconic symbols of the city's colonial heritage. These religious edifices, with their imposing facades and lavish interiors, represent the wealth and influence of the Catholic Church during the colonial period. The Church of São Francisco de Assis, designed by renowned architect Antônio Francisco Lisboa, known as

Aleijadinho, is a masterpiece of Brazilian Baroque architecture. Its intricate carvings, gilded altars, and magnificent ceiling paintings make it a must-visit attraction for art and history enthusiasts.

Ouro Preto is also renowned for its traditional festivals and cultural events. One of the most celebrated festivals is the Feast of Corpus Christi, which takes place in June. The streets of Ouro Preto come alive with vibrant processions, floral carpets, and religious ceremonies, attracting both locals and tourists who come to witness and participate in the festivities. The Carnival of Ouro Preto is another highlight, known for its lively parades, music, and street parties that showcase the region's rich cultural traditions.

The city is home to several museums that preserve and showcase Ouro Preto's historical and artistic treasures. The Museum of the Inconfidência houses artifacts and exhibits related to the Inconfidência Mineira, a movement for independence from Portugal that took place in the late 18th century. The Aleijadinho Museum displays the works and sculptures of the renowned artist, providing insight into his life and artistic legacy. These museums offer visitors an opportunity to delve deeper into the city's history and appreciate its cultural significance.

Ouro Preto's location amidst the picturesque landscapes of Minas Gerais adds to its allure. The surrounding hills, valleys, and waterfalls offer opportunities for outdoor activities such as hiking, exploring nature trails, and enjoying the scenic beauty of the region. Visitors can also venture to nearby historic towns, such as Mariana and Tiradentes, which share a similar colonial charm and provide additional insights into Brazil's past.

Preserving the city's historic character and cultural heritage is of utmost importance to Ouro Preto. Strict regulations and preservation efforts ensure that the city's architecture and cultural assets are safeguarded for future generations. This commitment to preservation has garnered international recognition and reinforces Ouro Preto's status as a cherished destination for those seeking a glimpse into Brazil's colonial history.

In conclusion, Ouro Preto stands as a remarkable testament to Brazil's colonial splendor. Its well-preserved historic center, magnificent churches, and rich cultural heritage invite visitors to immerse themselves in the grandeur of a bygone era. Ouro Preto's significance as a UNESCO World Heritage site and its commitment to preservation make it an essential destination for history and architecture enthusiasts, offering a captivating journey into the colonial past of Minas Gerais and Brazil as a whole.

# Fernando de Noronha: A Tropical Paradise

Fernando de Noronha, an archipelago located off the coast of Brazil, is renowned as a tropical paradise of unparalleled beauty. With its pristine beaches, crystal-clear waters, and vibrant marine life, it has captured the hearts of nature lovers, divers, and beachgoers from around the world.

Designated as a UNESCO World Heritage site, Fernando de Noronha is a protected marine park and ecological sanctuary. Its untouched natural landscapes and biodiversity make it a haven for wildlife and a mecca for conservationists. The archipelago consists of 21 islands, with the main island being the only inhabited one.

The beaches of Fernando de Noronha are nothing short of breathtaking. From the golden sands of Baía do Sancho, which has been voted the best beach in the world multiple times, to the secluded Praia do Leão with its pristine beauty, each beach offers a unique experience. Whether it's relaxing under the shade of palm trees, swimming in turquoise waters, or snorkeling among colorful coral reefs, the beaches of Fernando de Noronha captivate visitors with their natural splendor.

One of the archipelago's most iconic landmarks is Morro do Pico, the highest point on Fernando de Noronha. Hiking to the top rewards adventurers with panoramic views of the surrounding islands and the vast expanse of the Atlantic Ocean. The rugged cliffs and dramatic coastline add to the scenic allure of the island, creating photo-worthy moments at every turn.

Fernando de Noronha's marine ecosystem is a treasure trove of biodiversity. The surrounding waters are home to an incredible array of marine species, including sea turtles, dolphins, colorful fish, and even the majestic humpback whales that migrate through the area. Snorkeling and diving enthusiasts are treated to an underwater paradise, where they can explore vibrant coral reefs teeming with life and encounter fascinating sea creatures.

The archipelago's commitment to environmental preservation is evident in its strict visitor quotas and sustainable tourism practices. To protect the delicate ecosystem, the number of visitors allowed on the islands at any given time is limited, ensuring that the natural balance is maintained. Additionally, activities such as diving and snorkeling are closely regulated to minimize impact on the marine environment.

Beyond its natural wonders, Fernando de Noronha also offers cultural and historical attractions. The remnants of Forte Nossa Senhora dos Remédios, a 17th-century Portuguese fortress, stand as a reminder of the archipelago's colonial past. Visitors can explore the fort and learn about its historical significance in the defense of the region.

The local community on the main island of Fernando de Noronha is small and tightly knit. Residents take pride in preserving their island's natural beauty and welcoming visitors with warmth and hospitality. Sustainable practices and community involvement are key pillars of life on the archipelago.

To ensure the preservation of Fernando de Noronha's unique ecosystem and to provide a high-quality experience for visitors, access to the archipelago is regulated through an environmental preservation tax. This tax contributes to the conservation efforts and the maintenance of the island's infrastructure.

In conclusion, Fernando de Noronha stands as a tropical paradise of unparalleled beauty and ecological significance. Its pristine beaches, vibrant marine life, and commitment to environmental preservation make it a must-visit destination for those seeking a truly immersive and sustainable experience amidst nature's splendor. Whether basking on its stunning beaches, exploring its underwater wonders, or hiking to its panoramic viewpoints, Fernando de Noronha offers an unforgettable escape into a tropical paradise.

# Rio Carnival and Brazilian Festivals: Celebrating Life and Diversity

Rio de Janeiro Carnival, one of the world's most famous and vibrant festivals, takes center stage in Brazil's rich tapestry of cultural celebrations. Known for its exuberant parades, colorful costumes, and pulsating rhythms, the carnival embodies the spirit of celebration, unity, and joy that permeates Brazilian culture. However, Rio Carnival is just one of many vibrant festivals that take place throughout Brazil, each with its unique traditions and regional flavors.

The roots of carnival in Brazil can be traced back to Portuguese colonial times when European customs merged with African and indigenous influences. Over the centuries, these cultural elements fused to create a truly Brazilian celebration of music, dance, and revelry. Today, carnival is deeply ingrained in the national identity, showcasing the diversity and dynamism of the Brazilian people.

Rio de Janeiro Carnival stands out as a dazzling spectacle that attracts millions of visitors from around the world. The centerpiece of the carnival is the samba parade, a mesmerizing display of elaborate floats, vibrant costumes, and rhythmic samba dancing. The samba schools, representing different neighborhoods or communities, compete for the title of the year's best performance, pouring their hearts and souls into months of preparation. The energy and enthusiasm of the performers and spectators create an electrifying atmosphere that is truly infectious.

While Rio de Janeiro Carnival is undoubtedly the most famous, other cities across Brazil have their own unique carnival celebrations. Salvador, in the state of Bahia, hosts a carnival with a distinct Afro-Brazilian flavor. The streets come alive with the sounds of axé music and the rhythm of Afro-Brazilian drumming, as revelers follow the trio elétrico floats, dancing and singing their way through the city. Olinda and Recife, in the northeastern state of Pernambuco, offer a different carnival experience, known for their lively street parties, frevo music, and the traditional giant puppets called bonecos.

Beyond carnival, Brazil is a land of many other festivals that celebrate various aspects of the country's culture, religion, and traditions. Festas Juninas, held in June, are popular throughout Brazil and pay homage to the rural and agricultural heritage of the country. These festivals feature lively dances, traditional costumes, bonfires, and delicious foods like cornbread and canjica (a sweet corn pudding).

The Bumba Meu Boi festival in the northeastern region is a vibrant showcase of folklore, music, and dance. It tells the story of a resurrected ox and involves colorful parades, theatrical performances, and lively music that fuses indigenous, African, and European influences. The Parintins Festival, held in the state of Amazonas, is a unique spectacle featuring elaborate theatrical presentations by two rival groups known as boi-bumbás, who compete for the audience's favor with their intricate costumes, dances, and songs.

Religious festivals also play a significant role in Brazilian culture, blending Catholic traditions with indigenous and Afro-Brazilian beliefs. The Feast of Our Lady of Aparecida, the patroness of Brazil, draws millions of pilgrims to the city of Aparecida, where the Basilica of the National Shrine stands as a testament to the country's deep devotion. Círio de Nazaré in the city of Belém, Pará, is another major religious festival, honoring Our Lady of Nazaré and attracting devotees from all walks of life who join in a grand procession.

These festivals are not only an opportunity for Brazilians to celebrate their cultural heritage but also a chance to showcase Brazil's diversity, both regionally and ethnically. They reflect the country's history, traditions, and the fusion of its multicultural roots. From the rhythmic beats of samba to the pulsating drums of axé, from the vibrant costumes to the religious processions, Brazilian festivals are a vibrant mosaic of colors, sounds, and flavors.

In conclusion, Rio Carnival and Brazilian festivals exemplify the spirit of celebration, unity, and diversity that defines Brazilian culture. Whether it's the internationally renowned Rio de Janeiro Carnival or the local traditions of regional celebrations, these festivals are a manifestation of the Brazilian people's zest for life, their deep-rooted cultural heritage, and their desire to embrace and share their traditions with the world. The festivals are a testament to the country's rich tapestry of customs, music, dance, and religious beliefs, providing a glimpse into the soul of Brazil and its vibrant cultural mosaic.

# Conclusion

The history of Brazil is a tapestry woven with diverse threads, encompassing ancient civilizations, colonial conquests, economic booms, political struggles, and cultural transformations. From its indigenous roots to the arrival of the Portuguese explorers, the establishment of a colonial empire, the fight for independence, and the challenges of building a modern nation, Brazil's journey has been a complex and multifaceted one.

Throughout this book, we have explored the rich and vibrant history of Brazil, delving into the significant events, influential figures, and cultural milestones that have shaped the country. We have uncovered the indigenous cultures that predate European arrival, the waves of colonization that led to the establishment of a Portuguese dominion, and the subsequent struggles for independence and the formation of a new nation.

We have witnessed the rise and fall of economic booms, from the sugar and gold rushes to the coffee and rubber industries. These economic cycles brought both prosperity and challenges, shaping Brazil's socio-economic landscape and contributing to its complex identity.

The political history of Brazil has been marked by periods of stability, democratic governance, as well as instances of military rule and political repression. The quest for democracy and the struggle for social justice have played significant roles in the nation's development, culminating in the establishment of a democratic republic that continues to evolve to this day.

Brazil's cultural heritage is a kaleidoscope of influences, blending indigenous, European, African, and Asian traditions. From its literature, music, and cinema to its vibrant festivals and artistic expressions, Brazilian culture reflects the country's diverse heritage and serves as a unifying force that transcends regional differences.

The natural wonders of Brazil, from the Amazon rainforest to the Pantanal wetlands, the stunning coastline to the majestic waterfalls, showcase the country's ecological wealth and the need for environmental conservation. Brazil's biodiversity, encompassing countless species of flora and fauna, underscores the importance of preserving these natural treasures for future generations.

As we conclude this journey through the history of Brazil, it is important to recognize that no single book can capture the entirety of the nation's story. The chapters we have explored offer glimpses into different periods, aspects, and regions, but they are just fragments of a much larger narrative.

Brazil continues to evolve, facing challenges and embracing opportunities on its path forward. Its history serves as a foundation from which the country can learn, grow, and shape its future. The people of Brazil, with their resilience, creativity, and vibrant spirit, hold the key to the nation's continued development and progress.

As we close this book, may it serve as an invitation to delve deeper into the rich history of Brazil, to explore its diverse landscapes, and to engage with its vibrant culture. Let us appreciate the achievements, confront the challenges, and celebrate the multifaceted tapestry that is Brazil—a country of immense beauty, complexity, and potential.

Thank you for embarking on this journey through the history of Brazil with me. I hope that this book has provided you with valuable insights, deepened your understanding of Brazil's rich heritage, and sparked your curiosity to explore more about this fascinating country.

If you enjoyed this book and found it informative, please consider leaving a review on your preferred platform, sharing your thoughts and impressions. Your review will make a difference and contribute to the ongoing success of this book.

Once again, thank you for your time, interest, and support. I hope that the knowledge and experiences gained from this book will stay with you and inspire further exploration of the captivating history and culture of Brazil.

Made in the USA
Las Vegas, NV
01 June 2024

90603971R00066